The Power
of Alignment

The Power of Alignment

*How Great Companies Stay
Centered and Accomplish
Extraordinary Things*

GEORGE LABOVITZ   VICTOR ROSANSKY

John Wiley & Sons, Inc.
New York • Chichester • Weinheim
Brisbane • Singapore • Toronto

We dedicate this book to our parents, Janet and Jack Labovitz and Jennie and Joe Rosansky, who taught us the importance of being centered.

This text is printed on acid-free paper.

Copyright © 1997 by George H. Labovitz, Ph.D., and Victor I. Rosansky
Published by John Wiley & Sons, Inc.

All rights reserved. Published simultaneously in Canada.

Reproduction or translation of any part of this work beyond that permitted by Section 107 or 108 of the 1976 United States Copyright Act without the permission of the copyright owner is unlawful. Requests for permission or further information should be addressed to the Permissions Department, John Wiley & Sons, Inc.

This publication is designed to provide accurate and authoritative information in regard to the subject matter covered. It is sold with the understanding that the publisher is not engaged in rendering legal, accounting, or other professional services. If legal advice or other expert assistance is required, the services of a competent professional person should be sought.

Library of Congress Cataloging-in-Publication Data:

Labovitz, George H.
    The power of alignment : how great companies stay centered and
accomplish extraordinary things / George Labovitz and Victor Rosansky.
        p.   cm.
    Includes index.
    ISBN 0-471-17790-3 (cloth : alk. paper)
    1. Organizational change.   2. Strategic planning.   3. Information
technology—Management.   4. Competition.   I. Rosansky, Victor.
II. Title.
HD58.8.L3   1997
658.4′012—dc21   97-12815
                                                                      CIP

Printed in the United States of America

10 9 8 7 6 5 4

Contents

Acknowledgments

A number of individuals played an important role in the development of the conceptual framework of the alignment concept. A number of people, as well, helped us in the preparation of the text.

First we would like to acknowledge our colleagues at Organizational Dynamics, Inc., who shaped our ideas by sharing their own experiences as consultants and reviewing the text as it evolved. George Haskell made a real contribution by insisting that we keep refining the concept until he could understand it. Our U.S. colleagues Dave Dennen, Dick Gauthier, Alan Burleson, George Eckert, Jimmy Poole, Rocky Gaines, Dave Connaughton, and Dave Ebert; our European colleagues Manrico Mincuzzi, Luca Mortara, Alan

Robinson, Eileen Harrop, John Hutchinson, Nicola Diligu, and Paul Hesselschwerdt; and our Asian region colleagues Nic Thielson and Kevin Smith were generous with their time and insights. Our Boston University and ODI colleague and friend, Charlie Chang, has shared his wisdom with us for many years and has added measurably to our learning. It is a joy to work with such smart people.

The clients that we have worked with as we refined and implemented the alignment concept in their organizations are too numerous to name but are, in effect, our coauthors.

We would like to acknowledge the help we received in preparing the book from Dick Lueke, Tom Ehrenfeld, Jeremy Brown, Mark Brogna, Ellen Pfeiffer, and Karen Tehan. Joan Fallon, our assistant, was of great help, as well as being a conscientious and unerringly accurate typist and proofreader. Jim Childs and Jeanne Glasser at Wiley somehow managed to play both the role of caring critics and enthusiastic supporters at the same time. Their help was invaluable.

Lastly, we would like to thank our families for putting up with our absences during all those weekends. Without their support we never could have kept our day jobs and written a book at the same time.

All praise to these good people. Any lapses in logic are ours.

George Labovitz
Victor Rosansky

Preface

It is the custom of our company, Organizational Dynamics, Inc., to periodically hold client conferences. They are wonderful opportunities to celebrate successes and to share learning. Recently, at one of these, a client we have been working with for about three years related his extraordinary turnaround story. His company is a division of a major pharmaceutical company. At the time he took it over, it was generating about $50 million in sales and approximately $20 million in losses. He was sent by corporate with a clear charter—turn it around or shut it down. Three years later the division was generating $125 million and making $20 million in profit. It was a great story. At the bar that evening he turned to us and said, "I want you to know that I have learned one thing from you." "One thing?" we joked, "After three years, just one thing?" "Yes," he replied with great seriousness, "*Alignment is everything!*"

Our research and our experience have convinced us that growth and profit are ultimately the result of alignment between people, customers, strategy, and processes. We have found that organizations that consistently land on their feet during turbulent times are managed by people who keep everyone focused and centered around a few key business objectives. They do so in a way that creates a self-aligning and self-sustaining culture that distributes leadership and energy throughout their organizations and unleashes a kind of organizational power and focus that we call "alignment."

Alignment gives managers at every level of the organization the ability to

- Rapidly deploy a coherent business strategy
- Be totally customer focused
- Develop world-class people
- Continuously improve business processes—*all at the same time*

Air Force pilots are taught that in violent weather the secret of survival is to concentrate on attitude, altitude, and airspeed. The trick is to do so simultaneously, because they are all connected to each other. For example, if the pilot allows the aircraft to become "nose up" (attitude), the plane loses airspeed and is in danger of falling out of the sky. That lesson applies to organizations in turbulence as well.

The idea of focusing on several things at the same time requires the kind of systems thinking found in the work of authors such as Peter Senge. In systems thinking, the relationship between parts becomes as important as the parts themselves. Similarly, our concept of alignment is based on how an organization deals with customers, strategy, people, and processes as well as the relationship between them.

Our ideas about alignment evolved directly from the work we have been doing with clients in many different industries and operating environments. As we prepared this book, we interviewed a number of senior executives we have worked with who have used alignment to keep their organizations centered in the midst of change and who have generated sustained business results. We asked six CEOs, in particular, for in-depth interviews. They demonstrate the applicability of the concept across a broad range of businesses and provided us the wisdom that comes from successfully managing complex organizations in turbulent times.

Lee Cox, the recently retired president and CEO of AirTouch Cellular, created a culture of service and quality that he has leveraged to become a leader in the wireless communication industry. He maintained that focus and kept his organization centered while creating rapid growth in an industry that is undergoing pervasive and rapid change.

Daryl Ferguson, president of Citizens Utilities, together with Chairman Leonard Tow, has transformed a good company into a great one, as they have moved from traditional regulated energy business to a diversified telecommunication, cable, and energy business. In the last few years, they have grown from $360 million to over $1.3 billion, maintaining and improving on a 52-year track record of growth and profit.

Dennis O'Leary, M.D., president of the Joint Commission on Accreditation of Healthcare Organizations, has transformed the commission from a purely accrediting body for the 5600 U.S. hospitals into a service organization that is shaping the standards and ensuring the quality of comprehensive and integrated health care in this country.

Jim Orr, the chairman and CEO of UNUM Corporation, has guided his firm through the process of demutualizing, going public, repositioning their products and services, and creating a customer-focused culture that has transformed his firm into world leadership in disability, risk management, and insurance distribution.

Rick Scott, the chairman and CEO of Columbia/HCA Healthcare Corporation, built the number one health care provider in the United States. It owns or operates hundreds of hospitals, outpatient surgery centers, and other health care facilities throughout the United States, in the U.K., and in Switzerland.

Fred Smith, the chairman of Federal Express, is one of the most respected business builders and leaders in America. Our relationship with him goes back more than ten years. Throughout that time, we have learned far more from Fred than we have taught. His insights and knowledge have helped shape our concept of alignment.

Alignment is not a concept reserved only for senior management. We have seen supervisors and managers use it to unleash the power that comes from balance, focus, and the commitment of people to achieve a common goal—what we call the "Main Thing." Using the alignment concept, they have been able to establish a climate and culture that resulted in breakthrough levels of employee satisfaction, customer loyalty, and financial return.

Here are some key points to keep in mind when you are thinking about alignment:

- Alignment gives you the power to get and stay competitive by bringing together previously unconnected parts of your organization into an interrelated, easily comprehensible model.
- Alignment gives you the power to create an organizational culture of shared purpose.
- By integrating core business factors, market factors, overall direction, leadership, and culture, alignment gives your organization the power to achieve consistent, defined levels of growth and peak performance.

As we explain in the chapters that follow, getting aligned is simply the beginning of the game. That's because alignment is an ongoing process that requires constant, rapid realigning. Like flying, where the failure to make continuous heading corrections results in drift, organizations also wander from one side of their intended course to another. That's why frequent checking and realigning are so important. But with the right gauges and a crew that knows its business, you can stay on course. And that is what we'll show you how to do in this book.

There is an old story of a poor but righteous man who prayed every day and ended his prayer with the plea, "Lord, please let me win the lottery!" He never won. One day, toward the end of his life, he changed the end of his prayers by asking, "Lord, what must I do to win the lottery?" The clouds parted and the voice of the Lord said, "Give me a break . . . buy a ticket!"

We hope that you, too, will "buy a ticket" and unleash the power of alignment to achieve extraordinary results in your organization.

1

Getting to the Main Thing

"The *main thing* is to keep the main thing, the *main thing!*"

We loved that expression when we first heard it from Jim Barksdale, the CEO of Netscape, because that single sentence captures the greatest challenge that managers face today—keeping their people and organizations centered in the midst of change. There are two aspects to this challenge. The first is to get everyone headed in the same direction with a shared purpose. The second is to integrate the resources and systems of the organization to achieve that purpose—what we call the Main Thing.

We have been working with clients around the world for 25 years. In the 50 years of experience we both share, we have developed gray hair, no hair, and some insights about how to achieve business results in a world where the rules in the game of business are constantly changing. More than ever before, in our experience, we see that forces out of managements' control are affecting their ability to improve their team's and organization's performance.

We've watched them struggle as changes in the marketplace, technology, competition, and government regulations pull their organizations apart while all around them, the unrelenting pace of change—technological, competitive, and economic—continues to accelerate.

We've seen businesses traumatized by reengineering, downsizing, and "rightsizing." Like deer frozen in the headlights of a car, many organizations are stuck. There is an inertia that prevents them from moving in new, sometimes lifesaving, directions.

We have felt the frustration of managers as they try to "herd the cats" and get their people to work in concert with each other. No wonder so many of today's managers are *Star Trek* fans. They love it when the captain declares "Make it so!" because on *his* ship, as distinct from their own, something actually happens. The ship moves, the crew works together, the enemy is engaged, and the good guys win.

In an attempt to gain control over the forces swirling around them, to catch up to the pace of change, executives lurch from one management technique to another, only to find that instead of leading, they end up pushing.

THE AGE OF ALIGNMENT

- Imagine working in an organization where every member, from top management to the newly hired employee, shares an understanding of the business, its goals and purpose.

- Imagine working in a department where everyone knows how he or she contributes to the company's business strategy.
- Imagine being on a team whose every member can clearly state the needs of the company's customers and how the team contributes to satisfying those needs.

Sound impossible? It's not. The best organizations act this way and have accomplished extraordinary things. Your organization can do so by utilizing a new management approach. We call this approach *alignment*. We've put it to work in companies, hospitals, and government agencies around the world—with amazing results.

Alignment can be thought of as both a noun and a verb—a state of being and a set of actions. Alignment as a noun refers to the integration of key systems and processes and responses to changes in the external environment. But no organization can stay in a state of alignment for long, since almost every business lives in an environment of constant change. We think the real power of alignment comes when we view it as a set of actions—as a verb. These actions represent the new management competence, a necessary skill set that will enable managers to

- Connect their employees' behavior to the mission of the company, turning intentions into actions
- Link teams and processes to the changing needs of customers
- Shape business strategy with real-time information from customers
- Create a culture in which these elements all work together seamlessly

We have learned that outstanding executives do not simply inherit a culture; rather, they proactively create a self-aligning and self-sustaining culture in their organizations. That culture distributes leadership and energy throughout their organizations and unleashes a kind of power and focus that we call alignment.

We asked the outstanding executives we interviewed what the concept of alignment meant to them. Fred Smith, chief executive officer (CEO) of Federal Express, told us that "one of the first things we recognized is that most managers don't know what management is about. Alignment is the essence of management." Dr. Dennis O'Leary of the Joint Commission on Accreditation of Healthcare Organizations said, "Alignment ensures that the organization is in balance—that all the pieces fit together. I see the Joint Commission in what you are talking about . . . our accreditation process itself is consistently in search of organizational alignment. Alignment is what *we do*."

Lee Cox at AirTouch uses the analogy of a magnet to describe the impact of alignment. "If you drop a bunch of iron filings on a table from 10 feet, they'll be all over the place. Then as you start to put a magnet near them, you'll see the ones closest to the magnet start to move and twitch and start moving in the same direction. Getting into alignment is very difficult where there is none. Once you get there, staying in alignment isn't so difficult."

Lee's metaphor works for us. Like magnetism, alignment is a force. It coalesces and focuses an organization and moves it forward. Although they were unknown to each other, we had the advantage of knowing each of them. They all align their organizations by following the same deceptively simple steps:

- Carefully crafting and articulating the essence of their business and determining the Main Thing
- Defining a few critical strategic goals and imperatives and deploying them throughout their organizations
- Tying performance measures and metrics to those goals
- Linking these measures to a system of rewards and recognition
- Personally reviewing the performance of their people to ensure the goals are met

Although these steps seem deceptively simple, they are hard to implement and even harder to sustain.

WHY IS ALIGNMENT SO HARD TO ACHIEVE?

We are continually surprised to discover that, regardless of the country or the company, there exists a commonly shared "conspiracy" theory. It is a widely held belief that there must be some subversive force at work, some enemy, some competitor that is responsible for the confusion, inefficiency, and occasional stupidity that seem to occur in most organizations. How else could well-meaning people, members of the same organization who share common objectives and goals, end up inflicting such damage on each other? The answer is rooted in the very nature of traditional organizational design: "We have met the enemy, and it is us."

For centuries, whenever managers had a job to do, they instinctively recognized that the only way to manage it was to break it into pieces. The bigger the job, the greater the number of pieces. The only way to manage the pieces was to build a hierarchy of controls. Division of labor and span of control, therefore, are the primary pillars of classical organization.

Max Weber, the nineteenth-century German sociologist and economist, believed that bureaucracy was the most efficient form of organization. That might have been true for Max, but it is certainly not true for us. Something terribly dysfunctional happens when today's men and women are crammed into organizational designs that are thousands of years old. We don't fit!

Psychologists have long recognized that human beings relate to people who are like themselves and tend to reject people who are different from them. Yet organizations continue to create differences between people in the interest of efficiency. Line versus staff, management versus labor, field versus corporate, international versus domestic, East versus West, accounting versus sales—the list goes on. No wonder it's so hard to focus people around common goals when they are so different from each other simply by virtue of what they do and where they do it. Specialization and expertise can be a wedge that drives people further apart and makes it difficult for them to work together.

In the past, managers could rely on hierarchy, rules, and policies to exercise control. Today, because of constant change, traditional structures and controls are a liability. Where structure once served to create order and control, it now inhibits the organization's ability to respond to change in a rapid and focused way. Managers must now keep their people centered in the midst of change, deemphasize hierarchy, and distribute leadership by sharing authority, information, knowledge, and customer data throughout their organization.

Alignment is our response to the new business reality where customer requirements are in flux, competitive forces are turbulent, and the bond of loyalty between an organization and its people has been weakened. Aligned organizations capture the best of specialization but are able to respond quickly to change. People in aligned organizations have the capacity to sense change as it happens and the ability to realign themselves rapidly with a minimum of top-down direction. The old, linear approach has given way to one of simultaneity—to alignment.

THE ROAD TO EXCELLENCE

Many organizations have been on a road that has brought them closer to the kind of management we describe. Many are poised to take the final step to organizational alignment and by doing so achieve world-class levels of sustained excellence measured by financial, customer, and employee results. We've traveled that road with our clients. We've seen them become aware that the world has changed and that they are too bureaucratic, too inefficient, and too slow to compete effectively.

Often organizations have embarked on a path of enhancing organizational performance because they had to. In the late 1970s and early 1980s, the creation of a global economy brought with it the impact of global competition. The capability of the Japanese to build products of higher quality and at lower unit cost shocked and confounded American executives. They were slow to respond and even slower to recognize that dramatic, order-of-magnitude change was required if they were to compete—and survive.

Such lack of awareness is made painfully clear with this example. In the early 1980s, the new head of quality for one of the big three auto companies announced his department's five-year stretch goal: to reduce the number of cars rejected by their own quality control process from 6,000 per 100,000 to 1,000 per 100,000. True order-of-magnitude improvement, right? The trouble was that at the time Toyota's rejection rate was 48 per 100,000!

By the late 1980s and early 1990s, executives around the world woke up to the reality of global competition. Most responded with short-term, financially oriented solutions: they cut operating costs, increased sales of current products, and sold off marginal businesses.

As managers better understood their predicament, they realized that short-term patches would never cover the gaping chasm between their own practices and those of their most capable competitors. Imitation being the sincerest form of flattery, they began to learn from and emulate the Japanese. What they found, of course, was that much of what the Japanese were doing was following the advice and wisdom of Americans like Edwards Deming and Joseph Juran.

Beyond Total Quality Management and Reengineering

Total Quality Management (TQM) is both a framework that links the customer voice with a company's processes and a method for improving those processes, emphasizing continuous improvement and long-term cultural change. When introduced to American business, its purported benefits of lower costs and higher product/service quality made TQM attractive and timely. It was the perfect way to help organizations move from a newly awakened stage to a more active one.

Many organizations reported more activity than results. When we visited the headquarters of one of the largest electronics companies in Europe recently, we were told that they had been working on quality improvement since 1986. "If that's the case," we asked, "why have you asked us to come here?" The vice president of quality said, "Because nothing has happened! Nothing that the chairman can point to." Like many companies that attempted to implement TQM, they inadvertently fell into an "activity trap"—lots of teams working on lots of problems but with no connection to the Main Thing of the business.

Through the lens of alignment, we can see how sometimes TQM failed to create integration between customer requirements, process improvement, and overall organizational strategy. Because TQM focused on cycle time and defect reduction without a clear link to strategy, senior managers often failed to make the ongoing commitment critical to any TQM effort. The responsibility for quality was often delegated to quality zealots for whom short-term results became a goal unto itself. And while these enthusiasts tore through companies, senior managers turned their attention to what they considered to be more important matters— like technological change, government regulation, market share, or keeping up with global competitors. By assigning quality to a staff function, middle managers were disenfranchised from the process and from taking line responsibility for it.

The fault in many cases was not with the constructs and tools of TQM but with its implementation and the impatience of executives. Let's face it—steady incremental improvement is not something that rivets executive interest.

More recently, reengineering swept across the business landscape—a tidal wave that flooded many organizations, leaving behind a vast amount of wreckage. This method promised nothing short of dramatic gains in business performance; for executives impatient with the small but continual improvement of TQM, it held tremendous appeal. Hammer and Champy aimed to deliver dramatic performance gains in a single, bold stroke. "Reengineering, we are convinced, can't be carried out in small and cautious steps," they wrote in their book, *Reengineering the Corporation*, "It is an all-or-nothing proposition that produces dramatically impressive results."[1]

Like TQM, reengineering began with customers and worked back to the processes created to serve them. But its objectives were more limited than TQM's. It wasn't concerned with changing culture but with radically fixing ineffective processes. It ultimately was a mechanistic approach that yielded one-time gains that couldn't be sustained. Nothing in the reengineering process triggered continuous or sustained improvement.

Seen through the lens of alignment, it's clear that reengineering did not create linkages between different parts of the business. Perhaps its greatest weakness has been its utter disregard for people, both managers and workers alike. In a recent *Wall Street Journal* article, Michael Hammer pointed out that he and others had simply forgotten about people: "I wasn't smart about that. . . . I was reflecting my engineering background and was insufficiently appreciative of the human dimension."[2] People were moved around and, many times, out of companies as though they were pawns in a chess game. In many cases, companies have simply used reengineering as a convenient cover for the cost cutting they needed to produce short-term, bottom-line improvements.

Neither TQM nor reengineering are bad ideas. If implemented well, both can be useful tools for managers and will remain so for years to come. Each brings us further down the bumpy path toward performance improvement, but each fails to fully align the essential elements of the business to each other and to customers. Sustained excellence emerges when all the key elements of a business are connected to each other and are simultaneously linked to the marketplace.

Alignment provides a way of capturing the best of these two approaches by linking strategy and people and integrating them with customers and process improvement. Leadership and culture become the key drivers that enable an organization to adjust rapidly to its environment. They also ensure that everyone understands the Main Thing of the business. Takeo Shiina, the chairman of IBM Japan, summarized the difference well when he told us that "Alignment is not about the management of quality. It is about the quality of management."

ENDGAME: GROWTH, PROFIT, AND PERFORMANCE

"There are only two ways to make money in a business," according to the old adage. "You can raise the bridge or lower the river." In other words, increase revenue or cut costs. TQM and reengineering certainly focused on lowering the river. Today the focus must be on raising the bridge—on growth and profit. Companies that have tackled the issues of quality and competitiveness understand that cost and quality are commodities in the marketplace today, mere table stakes to play in the game. They need something else to differentiate themselves. To be industry leaders, they must become adaptive, flexible, and quick to respond to change.

Senior managers often ask us, "What should we be measuring to be sure our company is on the right track?" We answer their question with a question: "How do you know if any business is well run?" They invariably reply that a well-run business makes a profit and keeps customers and employees happy—in that order. We've asked this question hundreds of times and have always gotten the same answer. Until, that is, we met the senior management team at Federal Express in 1986.

At that meeting, the group responded to the question as we expected them to, until CEO Fred Smith demonstrated his understanding of alignment, stopping them and declaring, "not at Federal Express." He went on to explain that "we are in the service business. How can we deliver world-class service without world-class people? At FedEx," he said, "it must be

People-Service-Profit, in that order!" In other words, focus on your people and their ability to deliver world-class service. Profit is what you get if you do the first two things well. George Labovitz, a former U.S. Air Force pilot, then told Smith, a former Marine Corps pilot, about the F-105, a fighter bomber of the Vietnam era that the pilots called "The Thud." The manufacturer said it was a great airplane—it could fly fast, it could fly far, and it could carry a heavy bomb load. The pilots said that was true, but it couldn't do *all three things at the same time!* Similarly, the way to do all three things at the same time in a business is to focus on people and customers in order to get profit.

Fred Smith's insight and George's experience is confirmed by research conducted by James Heskett at the Harvard Business School. Heskett developed the concept of the service-profit chain. This concept holds that the endgame of business is growth and profit, which are tied to the ability of the organization to create customer loyalty and retention. These factors are then tied to customer satisfaction. Satisfaction depends on the organization's ability to deliver on its promise to customers, and that depends on employee loyalty and retention.

The link between people, customers, and profit and the interdependence among them was reinforced for us by Lee Cox at AirTouch. His company developed three overarching goals: customer satisfaction, employee satisfaction, and what they call 2 × 4, doubling the value of the stock in four years. He said, "By starting on day one with three goals that are in continual dynamic tension, it forced us to continually think about *simultaneously* achieving all three. . . . There's no such thing as having to compromise one for the other. Successful companies can do all three, and *we're* going to have to do all three."

This wisdom is sadly lost on many managers who have pursued growth and profits through cost-cutting and head-count reductions. Their companies may have seen an immediate gain, but they are now discovering the painful truth: You can't go on cutting costs and people forever. At some point, the road to long-term market and revenue growth must be found and rigorously followed. Many managers are discovering how hard it is to shift from cutting to growth, as the *Wall Street Journal* recently reported:

> Some companies, such as Airborne Freight Corporation, have tried to grow by cutting prices, only to ignite price wars. Some, such as Unisys Corporation, have tried to reposition themselves in faster growing industries, only to find competition so intense that profits are elusive. . . . One measure of the difficulty of going from cost cutting to revenue growing was a recent management study of 800 major U.S. companies. It found that 145 of them used cost cutting to reach profit levels above the industry average in the 1980s. But only 34, or 23 percent, made the switch to above average revenue growth as the catalyst for above average profits by 1995.[3]

Ultimately, if you want sustained growth and profit, if you want a company that is built to last, if you want to be among the industry leaders, you must create alignment between people, customers, strategy, and process.

Steve Rosedale is the founder of CommuniCare Health Services (CHS), a successful and rapidly growing long-term health care business in Ohio. We asked him a few questions: Why has he been able to achieve growth and profit in an industry where reimbursement is capped by Medicare and strangled by oppressive government regulation? Why is his turnover rate of staff so low when his competitors average between 80 and 110 percent turnover? Why is he able to be successful where so many others have failed? Here is his answer:

> The first thing we do is to define our business in a way that staff, patients, and payers can understand. We built our company with the mission of providing "life-giving days," and we try to find people who want to work with us in our commitment to patients and quality of care. What we have been able to do is to identify customer needs, employee needs, and company needs and align them. The staff invests time and clients invest money, as does the company. Therefore we are all stakeholders in ensuring that all of our units provide life-giving days. What we need from you is help in building the measures and process improvement capability that will help us grow. There is an old American Indian saying: "God gave to each people a cup of clay. From the cup they drank their lives." We have the essence; we need help in building the cup.

The chapters that follow will provide the concepts and methodology to enable you to construct your own cup: the systems, measures, and processes necessary to become aligned and to stay aligned. You can apply the concept and the approach to your entire organization or to any of its parts. We have seen supervisors and managers at every level use the power of alignment to unleash the energy that comes from balance, focus, and the commitment of people to accomplish the Main Thing.

2

Staying Centered:
What Alignment
Is All About

When Kmart, Wal-Mart, and Target, the three key players in the discount retail arena, squared off in the early 1990s, Kmart was the world's largest discount retailer. Five years later, Kmart had tumbled to third place and was in deep trouble. The appearance of its stores was lackluster. Stockouts were common, and employee morale was at rock bottom. 1995 revenues were only one-third those of Wal-Mart, the new retail kingpin.

What circumstances had pushed Kmart into the number-three spot? In a nutshell, while Wal-Mart was focusing on its core discount retail business and honing its buying and distribution systems, Kmart CEO Joseph Antonini was pursuing a diversification strategy aimed at acquiring specialty retail companies. Meanwhile, the jewels of the crown, Kmart's discount stores, lapsed into disorganization and disrepair. Customers began taking notice—*and* taking their business to Wal-Mart. By early 1995, 49 percent of Wal-Mart shoppers reported that their drive to Wal-Mart took them past a Kmart store.

Kmart's decline during the first half of the 1990s is symptomatic of a problem that afflicts many companies today—a failure to align the four essential elements that together create growth and profits: strategy, customers, people, and processes. In the past, we might have diagnosed Kmart's ills from one of several perspectives:

- Strategic: Kmart was following a poor strategy. It should have focused resources on its key assets: its discount stores.
- Quality: Kmart didn't take quality seriously. Neither its facilities nor its processes for delivering value to customers were up to standards.
- Reengineering: Kmart should have identified its customers, then, working backwards, redesigned its processes to serve them more effectively.

Each of the views just described is valuable, and each identifies an important part of the problem—but no single one can explain Kmart's fall from the top. And no one of these perspectives alone can suggest a complete remedy. This holds true for Kmart and for other companies that are losing the battle for growth and profits.

Focusing on strategy alone too often causes managers to view the business and its competitive environment as a high-level board game, to be won by moving assets around to defend turf or by taking advantage of opportunities or the weaknesses of rivals. It has little to say about the contributions of people and the way they work.

The quality approach, or TQM, is a way to continuously improve business processes. Its major flaw is that it too often diverts attention away from customers and important strategic issues. The TQM process can easily absorb everyone's attention. Florida Power & Light (FP&L), the first U.S. firm to win the coveted Deming Award, ran afoul of this fact. FP&L had established a 70-plus person quality department and had organized two-thirds of its employees into 1,900 quality teams. But, according to *The Economist*, "While customers saw some improvements in the quality of its services, these were insignificant when set against the sheer scale of the firm's quality effort. To a large extent, FP&L was simply going through the motions." Today, the legions of FP&L quality teams are gone, and the head of the company's downsized quality department is quick to affirm the centrality of the customer: "You have to keep going back to the customer to check what they want from you."[1]

On paper, at least, reengineering should bring companies back to their customers. After all, it begins with customers and works back through a succession of process steps. Reengineering does a good job of aligning the voice of customers with business processes. But experience shows that it loses touch with the people who are actually *doing* the work! In most cases, reengineering has left the few surviving people shell-shocked and alienated.

What is needed is a new way of looking at the challenge of growth and profitability—one that brings all important elements of the business into focus. This is the essence of alignment. Viewing Kmart from the alignment perspective, we see striking disconnections between the components that every business must coordinate to be successful. Antonini's diversification strategy changed the focus of managers and front-line employees from the needs and satisfaction of its core customers. In fact, most employees were clueless as to the real significance of their work. At the same time, the proven ways Kmart had used to deliver value to customers were seriously neglected. With these important aspects of its business out of alignment, it is little wonder that Kmart found itself in deep trouble.

To his credit, Antonini recognized the need to upgrade his stores, but the cash requirements for doing so forced him to divest many of the very businesses he had recently acquired. OfficeMax, Sports Authority, and Borders Group Bookstores all went back on the block. So much for the diversification strategy.

When Floyd Hall took over as CEO in June 1995, Kmart's situation was at rock bottom, and rumors of Chapter 11 lowered morale. The stock price was at a nine-year low. Wall Street analysts doubted Hall's ability to effect a turnaround. Indeed, at the time he was first considered for the CEO slot, Hall had not been in a Kmart or a Wal-Mart store for five years.

But Hall surprised the doubters. He put the retailer on the road to recovery. What made the difference? Hall began aligning key areas within his organization. He redirected strategy toward reviving Kmart's ailing core business. He hired 18 new executives and charged them with overhauling Kmart's disheveled systems for getting the goods to customers. To focus his managers' attention, Hall weighted executive pay with performance. Store managers had half of their annual bonuses tied to customer satisfaction.

Earnings rebounded as customers returned to Kmart. By the middle of 1996, Kmart was well down the road to recovery, and its stock price had rebounded 65 percent!

The Kmart saga illustrates the bad things that happen to a business when alignment breaks down and, conversely, the good things that happen when alignment is restored.

BALANCE AND FOCUS

If you've ever sat in the cockpit of a small plane as it makes its landing approach, you can appreciate the process of alignment. The pilot must sense and respond to a set of interactive variables that change as the plane makes its approach—with many things happening at once. Crosswinds affect the plane's orientation to the runway, which must be adjusted. Airspeed must be controlled with the flaps and throttle. The rate of descent, and pitch and yaw of the plane, too, must be adjusted as the plane moves down the glide slope. And there is substantial interaction among these many elements on landing. If the pilot manages them properly, the plane stays aligned with the runway and the glide slope, and it makes a safe landing.

Like landing an airplane, aligning a department or an entire organization is an ongoing balancing act that involves setting direction, linking processes and systems, and making *constant* adjustments. Fail to adjust and you'll drift. Overadjust and you'll lurch from one side of your intended course to another. The need for companies to reengineer is in many respects a consequence of past failures to make small, manageable adjustments on an ongoing basis.

Alignment relies on two essential dimensions: vertical and horizontal. The vertical dimension is concerned with organizational strategy and the people we rely on daily to transform strategy into meaningful work. The horizontal dimension involves the business processes that create what the customer most values.[2] As we'll soon show, both of these dimensions must be in sync—independently and with each other. Once alignment is achieved, performance measures and proper management are needed to keep it that way.

The idea of alignment is not new. Back in the late 1960s, Paul Lawrence and Jay Lorsch of Harvard Business School used the term "integration" to describe the state of collaboration that exists between departments that are required to achieve unity of effort by the demands of the environment.[3] Lawrence and Lorsch found that integrated organizations performed better in every measurable financial standard than did their nonintegrated counterparts. We favor the term "aligned" over "integrated" because it conveys direction as well as internal coherence.

FAST FORWARD: VERTICAL ALIGNMENT

Vertical alignment is about the *rapid* deployment of business strategy that is manifested in the actions of people at work. When vertical alignment is reached, employees understand organization-wide goals and their role in achieving them. This is not to say that every employee must be capable of explaining company strategy to Wall Street analysts, but everyone should be able to articulate the broader strategy and how his or her work is connected to it. The ultimate proof of vertical alignment is observable in the actions of front-line employees.

These actions are often striking. Employees of Southwest Airlines don't wear "We're Aligned" buttons, but they can tell you why everyone hustles to get their aircraft loaded, fueled, and into the air: Planes that sit at the gate don't make money. That is why Southwest's average flight turnaround time is only 15 minutes—one-third the industry average—even though its turnaround crews are half the size of its competitors.

With the goal of keeping its planes in the air clearly understood, just about anyone at Southwest Airlines can appreciate his or her part in the company's strategy. When they look at their work, they can identify and eliminate activities that needlessly keep planes sitting idly at the gate. "Our people," says CEO Herb Kelleher, "are ingenious at finding ways to do their jobs more easily and more productively."[4] For instance, SWA baggage handlers found that simply loading bags with handles out made unloading quicker and easier. Likewise, ticketing employees found that checking passenger reservation lists on less-than-full flights was an avoidable time waster.

> Vertical alignment energizes people, provides direction, and offers opportunity for involvement.

Federal Express is another company that has met the challenge of vertical alignment. After FedEx won the Baldrige Award in 1990, the Baldrige chief examiner took then Chief Operating Officer (COO) Jim Barksdale

aside and told him one reason the company had won
the award.

This examiner lived in Seattle. On the morning of his
trip to FedEx's Memphis headquarters, he decided to
begin the company's examination in his hometown, at
the FedEx airport drop-off booth.

The booth was attended by a smartly uniformed
young woman. As the examiner handed her a package
for delivery, he asked "I understand that your company is applying for a quality award of some kind?"

"Yes, sir," she replied, "the Baldrige Award. And I
think we have a good chance of winning it this year!"

"Do you do anything to improve quality yourself?"
he asked.

"Yes sir, I'm a member of a quality action team."

At the examiner's request, she explained the structure and the function of the company's quality teams
and described actions her team and others had taken
to reduce costs and improve employee and customer
satisfaction.

The examiner was impressed. The woman tending a
drop-off booth an entire continent away from FedEx's
Memphis headquarters clearly understood the company's goals and was involved in activities aligned
with them. She was one of over 120,000 FedEx employees but was knowledgeable and involved with the corporate imperatives of "People, Service, Profit."

Vertical alignment implies more than employee
compliance with strategy that is set at the top. It's a
two-way street. Strategy must be determined by customers, but it must also be informed and shaped by
the people who implement it. Employees in the middle of the organization and on the front lines almost
always experience greater intimacy with customers

and competitors than do senior managers, and their insights can enrich strategy—but only if they are actively solicited. That's what we mean by a two-way street. Executives who create strategies in the isolation of their 20th-floor offices inevitably discover that their strategies do not match up with the environment of the street-level employees. To avoid a disconnect, there must be continual feedback between the two (Figure 2-1). (We'll spell out the details in Chapter 4.)

Stellar Performance

A great example of how a company listened to both its customers *and* its employees in strategy development comes from Jet Propulsion Laboratory (JPL). JPL videotaped conversations with key customers concerning their requirements and what they expected JPL to provide. At the same time, they videotaped managers and employees discussing what they saw as the future of the company, its strengths and weaknesses. These videos were shown throughout JPL facilities and used as a catalyst to discuss how to change to meet customer and stakeholder needs. The result was a dramatic improvement in customer satisfaction.

The late Sam Walton understood the importance of this vertical feedback mechanism as much as any executive we have known. The phrase "vertical feedback mechanism" was not in Sam's vocabulary, but the concept was in his bones. Like McDonald's founder, Ray Kroc, Sam Walton had a passion for being in his stores—walking around; looking at the displays; and talking

Strategy

People

Figure 2-1. Vertical alignment.

with customers, employees, and store managers. The richest man in America (at the time) genuinely wanted to know what floor clerks making slightly above the minimum wage knew better than he. "What's moving?" he would ask them. "What are customers asking for today? What do you think of this floor display?"

It's doubtful that senior executives at Kmart shared Sam's passion for the ground floor. If they had, they never would have let their stores appear run-down or second-rate. Instead, they would have lavished their time and attention on the stores—as Sam did—instead of on the acquisition game. And they certainly would have had the input of employees.

Beyond Slogans and "Corporate-Speak"

Getting employees at all levels to buy into company strategy requires more than memos, corporate "town meetings," and slogans. It requires a serious and demonstrated commitment—something Ford Motor Company learned the hard way.

In the automobile business, the term "job one" refers to the first car coming off a new production line. Getting that car as perfect as possible is an important operational goal. In the early 1980s, Ford expanded this term to "Quality Is Job One," implying the overriding importance of quality in everything done by the company. It was an exceptional concept and quickly found its way into the company's advertising. Ford management was so excited by the slogan that they put it on hats, buttons, tote bags, and jackets.

Rank-and-file Ford workers were less excited. In fact, some wouldn't be caught dead wearing or carrying anything that said "Quality Is Job One." Why? To them it was just a bogus slogan cooked up by the company's advertising people. They simply didn't believe that management was committed to the proposition of quality. Indeed, they had grounds for disbelief. Product quality had not been Ford's strong suit during the 1970s. Its vehicles by that point had earned it the acronym FORD: Fix Or Repair Daily.

But Ford management *had* gotten the message about product quality and *was* serious; it simply hadn't demonstrated its commitment to the people on the line. Only time and ongoing support for quality training and programs succeeded in convincing the rank and file of the company's commitment to "Job One." Once that happened, people got on board and quality at Ford became a reality. They formed quality teams, line workers got involved in product design, and "Job One" was no longer a slogan. Before long, Ford became the most profitable of U.S. automakers, outstripping its larger and long-time rival, General Motors.

CROSSING BOUNDARIES: HORIZONTAL ALIGNMENT

Vertical alignment alone will not yield sufficient growth and profits. Companies that sustain a position of industry leadership must make an absolute commitment to their customers. That commitment pervades every aspect of their business and the way they meet customer requirements. In these organizations, L.L. Bean's famous dictum that "the customer is not an interruption of our work" sets the agenda.

Over the past decade, companies have learned how to improve—or even reengineer—the processes through which they meet or anticipate customer requirements. Because these processes generally cut across different functions of the company, they are called "horizontal." We use this term in a higher sense—one that goes beyond process management and links customer requirements with the way we do business (Figure 2-2). It's necessary that people work together across varying activities and functions, but it is also necessary that they work on the *right* things. This must be determined by customers. Unfortunately, the customer voice is often lost beneath other, louder sounds: departmental reorganizations, the budgeting process, office politics. You know the story.

Bringing the Customer Inside

The antidote is to get up close and personal with your customers. Aligned companies don't rely solely on traditional market research to understand what customers want. They eliminate the boundaries between

Processes ◄─────────────────► Customers

Figure 2-2. Horizontal alignment.

themselves and their customers. In effect, they bring their customers inside, making them participants in their company's value-creating processes.

Martin Marietta Corporation did just this with the U.S. Navy, one of its biggest buyers of electronic instruments. Up to this point, any problem with an electronic product resulted in a massive exchange of paperwork between the navy and Martin Marietta. The problem had to be documented and discussed. Resolution often took months, wasted time and energy, and created frustration for both parties. This procedure followed the old "inspect and accept or reject" approach to quality control that Juran, Deming, and others have taught us to eliminate.

Eventually, Martin Marietta found a better way: It invited navy personnel to participate in its design and production meetings. Such participation meant that the navy's requirements would be met the first time. It also provided an opportunity to clarify the navy's product specifications early in the process.

(In Chapter 5 we'll show you some techniques for getting clearer signals from your customers [even your worst critics], discovering their *root* needs, and identifying opportunities to delight them.)

Getting to the Core

Understanding what customers really want is only half the battle for achieving horizontal alignment. The other half is follow-through—creating and delivering what your customers want, when and how they want it! Today it is almost universally understood that this is accomplished through the right business processes. The best companies align their processes with customer requirements and then work constantly at improving them. Most of the organizations that have stalled in their progress toward superior performance have mastered local or departmental processes, but not the cross-functional processes that lead to customer satisfaction and retention. In other words, they have mastered the easier, smaller processes, but not the big ones that matter most.

Why does this happen? We sometimes explain it with this story. A man was driving down the highway in his Volkswagen Beetle when a Ferrari blew past him, practically forcing him off the road. "You @#?$#!" he cried as he regained control of his car.

Putting his foot to the floor, the VW driver gave chase, straining to reach his top speed of 60 miles per hour. Suddenly, the flashing lights of a police car appeared in his rear-view mirror, and he was forced to pull over.

"Sir," the policeman told him, "You were driving faster than the posted speed limit of 55 miles per hour. I'll have to give you a ticket."

"Me?" stammered the driver in disbelief. "You're giving *me* a ticket? Didn't you see that Ferrari? He must have been going at least 120 miles per hour. Why are you giving me a ticket instead of him?"

"Because, I can't catch the Ferrari."

Like the policeman, we tend to go after the small problems we can catch and solve easily, but we leave the larger, more critical problems alone.

THE DYNAMIC DUO:
WHEN BOTH DIMENSIONS ARE ALIGNED

So far, we have described two dimensions of alignment: vertical and horizontal. Now these must be brought into alignment *with each other*. Neither a great strategy nor the full commitment of managers and employees will have the right result if a company's processes for creating and delivering value have targeted the wrong customers—or worse, if they have targeted the right customers with the wrong product. Examples here are abundant: Polaroid's attempt to displace traditional movie film with "instant" Polarvision, RCA's ill-fated videodisc, and the "new" Coca-Cola.

Nor will the company that is fully aligned on the horizontal dimension succeed if its strategy or implementation is flawed. Apple Computer may have fallen afoul of these important principles. Its Macintosh computers are highly reliable and easy to use. Customers love them and are fiercely loyal. Try to replace an employee's Mac with a PC and you'll likely get your hands slapped. Yet the company has captured only 10 to 12 percent of the personal computer market. The company's early strategy of retaining sole rights to the Macintosh operating system no doubt has led to its failure to make larger waves in the market. Neither technical product superiority nor customer loyalty has helped it.

When alignment is achieved in both dimensions, as demonstrated in Figure 2-3, a dynamic relationship exists between all four elements. When the four elements of alignment are simultaneously connected with each other, each element is supported and strengthened by

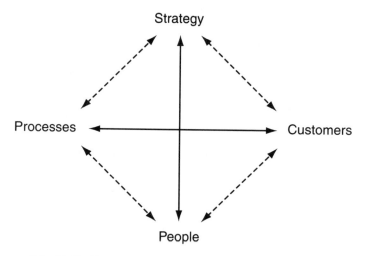

Figure 2-3. Full alignment.

the others. The full power of alignment is unleashed, and great things happen. The organization has great resilience and agility. It moves and adapts with catlike speed. When it hits a wall, it can pick itself up and move on.

Dr. Dennis O'Leary gave us a perspective about alignment that we hadn't thought of. What happens if you aren't aligned? In his business, those health care organizations that fail to meet the standards are less likely to be enthusiastic supporters of the Joint Commission. He said, "If a health care organization that we accredit isn't aligned, it is vulnerable and so are we. In our line of work, we don't attract much popular appeal; we're the big health care quality overseer that people like to knock down. So alignment has some very practical meaning for me. When an accredited organization becomes aligned, because its accreditation lies in the balance, it's our greatest defense; it's the reason we're successful."

With both the vertical and horizontal dimensions aligned, your strategy and your people are synchronized with customer focus and process capabilities. Consider what would happen if a new technology substantially increased demand for a product or service provided by a fully aligned company. As the strategy to meet this need was formulated, market data would be analyzed to determine the optimal way to meet customer needs. At the same time, process capabilities would be reviewed and adjusted to ensure that they could meet those needs. When the strategy was executed by employees, it would naturally bring with it all of the customer and process information that had contributed to its formulation. All of the people in the company would help carry out the strategy in some way, and each would be linked to the company's customers and processes (Figure 2-4). Customer focus, people, and processes are each enriched by the elements to which they are linked through alignment.

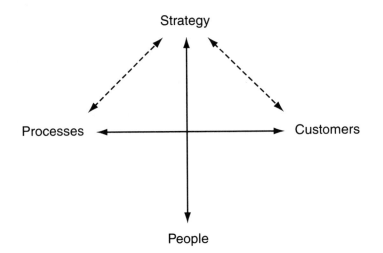

Figure 2-4. Processes and customer focus impacts strategy and its deployment.

THE COCKPIT VIEW

So how do we get and *stay* aligned?

Earlier we used the analogy of landing a small airplane to describe the challenge of getting and *staying* aligned when many factors are changing at once. Most airports and aircraft now have an electronic system that helps pilots in this difficult task, especially when visibility is poor. Called the ILS (Instrument Landing System), it helps the pilot align vertically and horizontally with the runway during the approach. Radio transmitters send one signal along the center axis of the runway and another signal along the required glide path. Cockpit receivers pick up the ILS signal and indicate whether the plane is too high or too low given its distance from the runway and whether its course is aligned with the runway or at an angle to it. (Figure 2-5 is similar to the ILS indicator found in a cockpit.)

The instrument in the top panel indicates that the plane is too high. By lowering the nose of the plane, the pilot will see the horizontal bar move up toward the center. The vertical bar indicates that the plane is too far to the left, and the pilot must turn the plane right to get aligned with the runway. When both bars are crossed in the center, as in the bottom panel, the plane is on the proper glide path for a safe landing.

Crosswinds, airspeed, rate of descent, and other factors all conspire to move the plane off this perfect course. So the pilot has to keep adjusting altitude and direction all the way down to the runway.

If aligning a company, a department, or a work team were as straightforward as setting up a good landing, we'd all be aces. It's a challenge requiring simultane-

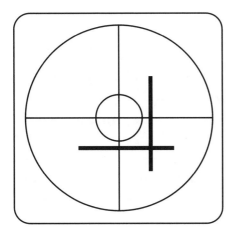

Out of alignment:

Left of runway
Altitude too high
(above glide path)

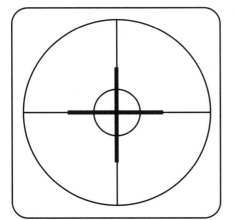

In alignment:

Aligned with the runway
At the right altitude
(on glide path)

Figure 2-5. Landing with the ILS.

ous matching of both vertical and horizontal aspects of the business, as well as of external elements—suppliers, partners, and so forth. In the end, all of these elements must be centered on the ultimate objective of the business. We call this objective *the main thing*.

THE MAIN THING

You don't have an instrument panel on your desk, but you surely have gauges of performance that indicate what's going on in your business: financial and production reports, customer-satisfaction measures, sales per employee, product defects per thousand, economic value added, and dozens of others. In fact, the information that most managers have today is often overwhelming.

Good managers, like good pilots, understand that some measures are more important than others, and they concentrate on these. Like the ILS indicator, they give the manager a sense of alignment and an ability to identify where adjustments are needed. We'll get into these measures later in the book. For now, we'll simply say that these measures should all point to the main thing of the business.

Every organization has a main thing—the single most powerful expression of what it hopes to accomplish, its instrument for producing growth and profits. Growth and profits are surely the ultimate aim of any business organization, but they are *outcomes* of succeeding with the main thing. Fred Smith, CEO of Federal Express, described to us his concept of the main thing—what he calls the "theory of the business."

Every successful business has, at its heart, a theory of the business—an underlying set of supporting objectives and a corporate philosophy that gives people a foundation on which to operate. Working inside that framework, they've got an idea of what we want them to do—to prioritize. We [at FedEx] have a very clear business mission and a business theory which is understood certainly by every member of the management team, and probably by 90 percent of the workforce.

For Smith and FedEx, the main thing is absolutely reliable express delivery. Customers will pay a premium for reliable express delivery because it is extremely important to them, and FedEx cannot afford to disappoint them.

For the late Sam Walton, founder of Wal-Mart, the main thing was, in his words, "the box" and its presentation. The box was the store and everything about it: the employee who greets each customer at the door, the merchandise displays, and the helpfulness of store personnel. Take care of the box, Walton used to say, and you'll take care of the business.

For McCaw Cellular, according to former CEO Jim Barksdale (now CEO of Netscape), the main thing was retaining subscribers—something he quickly recognized on taking charge of the company. In a business plagued by high customer churn (turnover), Barksdale recognized that continuity of subscribership was the key to business achievement. That's why he kept McCaw employees focused on one key indicator: customer churn rate. By concentrating on the churn rate and keeping it low, McCaw managed to reverse its flagging performance within six months.

We recently came to know Les McCraw, the chairman of Fluor Corporation. He has guided his company's subsidiary, Fluor Daniel, to become one of the leading engineering, construction, and diversified service companies in the world. At Fluor Daniel, the central thrust of the main thing is safety. With the entire company focused on the main thing, Les believes that safety reflects the ability of "managers to manage and leaders to lead." He feels that this safety discipline in turn positively impacts cost, quality, and schedule achievements. Fluor Daniel's focus on safety has resulted in a lost work-time case rate that is 54 times better than the national average for the engineering and construction industry. With safety keeping it centered, Fluor Daniel has become the safest company of its type in the world.

George Hennigan, president of Kerr-McGee Chemical Corporation, told us a similar story. In 1988, his company experienced three fatalities. The incidents shocked and galvanized George to make safety the main thing at Kerr-McGee Chemical. He created an Executive Safety Committee that meets monthly, and he requires every senior executive to attend. Since 1988, George has not missed a single meeting.

George and the senior managers also visit each production facility to hold safety awareness seminars. By making safety the main thing at Kerr-McGee, and following through with proactive senior management involvement, they have driven their work safety incidents to zero in 13 of their 17 plants during the last five years. OSHA has named Soda Springs, Idaho, home of Kerr-McGee's vanadium plant, the safest chemical work location in the world.

The prime minister of Malaysia, Dr. Mahathir Mohamad, provides one of the most impressive examples of focusing on the main thing—except that he is using the concept to align an entire *country!* Dr. Mohamad, recognized as one of Asia's leading statesmen, has declared that by the year 2020, Malaysia will be a world-class industrial nation. To achieve Malaysia's main thing, he has mandated the use of TQM throughout the government and has sought the collaboration of Malaysian industry. One of our clients, the Hong Leong Group Malaysia, a 40,000-person conglomerate led by visionary chairman, Quek Leng Chan, answered Dr. Mohamad's call for corporate partners. Mr. Quek has aligned his company's strategic goals with that of his country and now uses the strategy deployment process (described in Chapter 4) to ensure that every one of the 100-plus companies of the group is in sync with the corporate and country vision to be world class.

The result? In December 1996, the Hong Leong Group Malaysia was named one of Asia's leading companies by "The Review 200," a survey conducted by the *Far Eastern Economic Review*.[5] Ranking was based on leadership, recognizing companies that provided high-quality products and services, were innovative in customer response, had a long-term vision, exhibited financial soundness, and that other companies would emulate. Chairman Quek's determination to build a world-class company ensures that Malaysia's main thing is well on its way to being achieved.

What is your main thing?

The Main Thing

- The main thing for the organization as a whole must be a common and unifying concept to which every unit can contribute.

(Continued)

(Continued)
- Each department and team must be able to see a direct relationship between what it does and this overarching goal.
- The main thing must be clear, easy to understand, consistent with the strategy of the organization, and actionable by every group and individual.

When people ask us how to align the four elements of performance—and keep them aligned—our short answer is *focus on the main thing* (Figure 2-6). This means continually thinking about strategy, processes, people, and customers; and how each should be adjusted to get you to the main thing.

The main thing is to the manager and the employee what the runway is to the pilot during the landing. It's

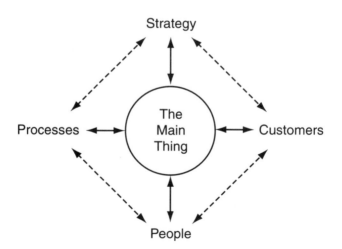

Figure 2-6. Focus on the main thing.

what he or she must focus on, manipulating each of the other elements as needed to keep aligned. So we ask

"Is our strategy the best it could be for optimizing the main thing?"

"Do our people understand the strategy and have the proper training and incentives to work for the main thing?"

"Are our processes and the ways in which we deal with customers linked to the main thing?"

CENTERING PEOPLE: ALIGNMENT AT EVERY LEVEL

It would be easy to think that everything we've said so far about alignment is for senior managers only. On the contrary, the activities and behavior of people at *every level* must be aligned with the main thing. When this happens, tremendous organizational power is created. The energy of the many is focused in a single direction. In its absence, energy is dissipated; the organization is like an engine whose cylinders are not firing at the right time or in the proper sequence. This is why middle and lower-level managers need to be as aware of alignment as the people at the top.

Philips Electronics, a multinational company, determined that it was critical to put a sense of urgency into its efforts to reduce costs and improve its operating efficiency. To do this, it aligned and focused the organization by setting aside one day during which more than a hundred thousand employees around the world were to initiate specific projects. The key to the effort's success, and the innovation borne from it, was the sheer excitement and focus engendered by getting so many people working simultaneously on the same thing.

In order to check how well people are aligned in your organization, try the "Elevator Test." The next time you get on an elevator, ask the person on your left or right three questions after the door closes: "What is the strategy of this organization?" "What do you do?" and "How does what you do support the strategy?" When we use the elevator test as "out house" consultants, we find that most people have a good idea of what they do but often don't have a clue about the organization's strategy and how their job connects to it.

It is easy for employees in big companies with functional departments to lose sight of what Fred Smith calls "the theory of the business," or to confuse it with preparing financial statements, or creating marketing plans, or writing programs for the Management Information Systems (MIS) department, or whatever. Employees need to see the larger purpose in their particular jobs and their connection to the main thing. That is why managers at every level—from top to bottom—must be concerned with alignment.

"How aligned is your company or work group?"

"Is the main thing clear?"

"Has strategic intent been translated into work that people have been trained and rewarded to do?"

"Are core processes designed to deliver what customers really want?"

These are the questions you should be asking yourself as you move forward. The next chapter provides a mechanism you can use to answer these questions. And it describes the typical pathologies that keep many organizations out of alignment.

3

Organizational Pathologies

Medical doctors use the term "pathology" to refer to the origin and nature of disease in the human body. As organizational doctors, we use the same term when we refer to the maladies that keep businesses from achieving their intended purposes: growth and profitability. Organizational pathologies, like their biological counterparts, have symptoms and causes. And, as you'd expect, the symptoms reveal themselves more easily than do the causes.

Most of us are familiar with the symptoms of ailing growth and profitability:

- Customer dissatisfaction
- Declining market share
- Poor morale
- Turf warfare
- Inefficient processes
- A chronic inability to improve
- A lack of consensus on ends and means

Companies with these symptoms produce disappointing results and are not fun places to work. The causes behind these symptoms are often traceable to alignment problems in which one or more of the four key elements of the organization—strategy, customer focus, employees, or processes—is being overlooked.

A DIAGNOSTIC TOOL

The symptoms of dysfunction call for a method for diagnosing the cause or causes. Several years ago we developed the Alignment Diagnostic Profile (Table 3-1) for this purpose. It is designed to give organizations a visual and quantitative measure of their alignment with respect to strategy, customers, people, and processes. This tool has been refined over the years, based on continued learning, and we've administered it to thousands of people in scores of organizations. It simply presents each individual with a series of statements and asks them to indicate how their organization's behaviors and practices measure up against each. They assign a number—from 0 through 10—indicating how strongly they disagree or agree with each statement. The short version of the questionnaire and the scoring scheme, with hypothetical scores, is shown in Table 3-1. Here, 0 equals strong disagreement and 10 equals strong agreement. Most responses, as you might guess, fall somewhere between the extremes.

How would you score your company in terms of each of these 16 statements? How would your colleagues (or the people who work under you) respond?

Table 3-1. Alignment Diagnostic Profile (short version).

Strategy	Strongly disagree		Strongly agree

Strategy

Organizational strategies are clearly communicated to me.
0 1 2 3 4 5 6 (7) 8 9 10

Organizational strategies guide the identification of skills and knowledge I need to have.
0 1 2 3 4 5 (6) 7 8 9 10

People here are willing to change when new organizational strategies require it.
0 1 2 3 4 (5) 6 7 8 9 10

Our senior managers agree on the organizational strategy.
0 1 2 3 4 5 6 (7) 8 9 10

Total [25]

Customers

For each service our organization provides, there is an agreed-upon, prioritized list of what customers care about.
0 1 2 3 4 (5) 6 7 8 9 10

People in this organization are provided with useful information about customer complaints.
0 1 2 3 (4) 5 6 7 8 9 10

Strategies are periodically reviewed to ensure the satisfaction of critical customer needs.
0 1 2 3 4 (5) 6 7 8 9 10

Processes are reviewed regularly to ensure that they contribute to the attainment of customer satisfaction.
0 1 2 (3) 4 5 6 7 8 9 10

Total [17]

People

Our organization collects information from employees about how well things work.
0 1 (2) 3 4 5 6 7 8 9 10

My work unit or team is rewarded for our performance as a team.
0 1 2 3 4 5 6 7 (8) 9 10

(Continued)

Table 3-1. Alignment Diagnostic Profile (short version) (*Continued*)

People (*con't.*)	Strongly disagree										Strongly agree
Groups within the organization cooperate to achieve customer satisfaction.	0	1	2	3	4	⑤	6	7	8	9	10
When processes are changed, the impact on employee satisfaction is measured.	⓪	1	2	3	4	5	6	7	8	9	10

Total [15]

Processes

	Strongly disagree										Strongly agree
Our managers care about *how* work gets done as well as about the results.	0	1	2	3	4	⑤	6	7	8	9	10
We review our work processes regularly to see how well they are functioning.	0	1	2	3	4	5	⑥	7	8	9	10
When something goes wrong, we correct the underlying reasons so that the problem will not happen again.	0	1	2	3	4	5	⑥	7	8	9	10
Processes are reviewed to ensure they contribute to the achievement of strategic goals.	0	1	②	3	4	5	6	7	8	9	10

Total [19]

©1996 *Organizational Dynamics, Inc.*

We have assigned hypothetical scores to Table 3-1 in order to demonstrate the next step of the diagnosis: mapping. Here we take our alignment frame, assign a 0 to 40 scale along each dimension, mark each with the respective score, and connect the dots. The result is a snapshot of the organization's alignment, as shown in Figure 3-1. The hypothetical scores shown in the diagnostic tool

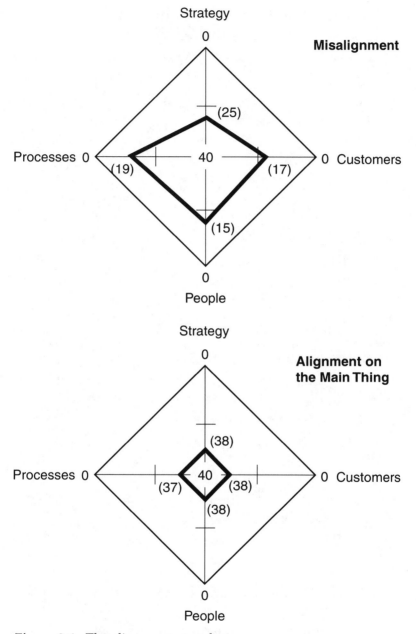

Figure 3-1. The alignment snapshot.

are reflected in the top panel of the figure. The picture we'd *like* to see is in the bottom panel. Using the 0–40 scale, 40 is the highest score you can achieve.

The Extended Alignment Diagnostic Profile

The short version of our diagnostic tool has several benefits: for respondents, it is easy to understand, score, and interpret. And it is an effective way to reveal the larger misalignment problems. It is incomplete, however, since it considers only the internal environment of the firm. In our consulting work, we generally use an extended version of this same tool. The extended version asks individuals to respond to a more robust set of statements and expands the set of internal dimensions to include leadership and culture. It also measures the organization's responsiveness to its external environment—competition, technology, regulation, and economics. For example, it asks the respondent to agree or disagree with statements such as: "I have access to up-to-date information on competitive issues that affect the work I do." This expanded set of statements and responses allows us to develop a more complete diagnosis.

COMMON ORGANIZATIONAL MALADIES

Years of practice help medical doctors quickly recognize common patterns in ill or injured patients. Organizational maladies likewise exhibit patterns, and we will share a few of the more common ones with you. This list is by no means complete, but it captures the main pathologies seen in misaligned companies.

Pathology 1: The Tyranny of One

Not so long ago, a major U.S. food company introduced an improved version of one of its long-standing products, canned refried beans. The original version had been on the market for a number of years and had established an acceptable market share. Hoping to expand this share, the company's marketers did extensive research, including taste tests with focus groups. Acting on that research, product developers and the manufacturing group diligently formulated what all hoped would be an improved product. Each group was satisfied that it had done its job extremely well. The new and improved beans were launched with generous promotional support and high expectations.

Initial sales of the new product were right in line with the company's expectations but soon began to slump on a monthly basis. Hoping to reverse flagging sales, the company poured more resources into promotion, but with little success. Everyone asked "What's going on?" Follow-up studies with customers indicated that the consistency of the reformulated refried beans was disagreeable.

Every department that had a hand in the project felt that it had done its job right. And before long, the blame game was in full swing. "Our market research was inadequate." "The product developers made the beans too thin." "Manufacturing doesn't have its processes properly tuned."

In fact, each department had done its job and, in terms of its own criteria, had done it very well. But the combined result of their efforts had left customers unsatisfied. We call this common pattern the tyranny of one because each group did the best job it knew how to do based on its own understanding of "best." No group, however, attempted to understand its contribution based on the customer's experience of the product.

The tendency for each department to focus on its own results while failing to make the most of the result for the customer is one of the ironies of organizational life. In this particular case, the antidote was to develop an incentive system that tied compensation for members of the different functions to two measures of customer satisfaction. Once that system was in place, people's behavior changed for the better, and they started aligning their efforts with the customer.

Pathology 2: Strategy Interruptus

Many organizations develop great strategies that simply go nowhere. Their intentions never get below the neckline; their strategies are never implemented.

The quality of the strategy is certainly important, but quality doesn't matter when strategy is ignored. We can say with confidence that a company is better off with a B-rated strategy and an A-rated implementation than the reverse.

You can probably tell that we are not strategy purists. To us, the definition of good strategy is subjective. In any case, it is always subject to adjustment as the competitive environment changes. That's why it's important to come up with a *good* strategy and deploy it *quickly.*

The failure to execute strategy quickly can usually be traced back to the way it was formulated. Too often, a small group of people spend a great deal of time formulating a strategy, with much less attention given to its implementation. They create the strategy, then direct everyone else to support it. This support is withheld for all of the obvious reasons: the implementors have no ownership of the strategy; they are not privy to the thinking that went into it. It's not surprising, then, that so many people—including senior managers—interpret strategy to fit what they are already doing. Lacking buy-in, there is no alignment, and strategy is just a deadweight.

We once consulted for an electric utility company that had a fully developed strategy and a nicely printed booklet that explained it to employees. A series of briefings had been held with middle managers to get them on board. But nothing was happening with the strategy. Even some of the senior managers were ignoring it.

The problem, as we quickly discovered, was that a gap existed between the strategy and its implementation. No one could see a context for the strategy, the main thing it served, or how they could contribute to it. The strategy was viewed as an intellectual contrivance, and it failed to inspire or connect with people's work. No one had bought in.

We helped this company and its employees relate their strategy to the main thing of the business. Once people got the picture, they could see the sense of the strategy and how they could contribute.

Pathology 3: The Phantom-Limb Syndrome

People who have had the misfortune of losing a limb often feel as though the limb is still there. They continue to envision the limb and feel sensations in it. In one account, a man felt that he could wiggle the toes on a foot he had lost years before. Physiologists call this the phantom-limb syndrome and explain it in terms of imprinted memories. The brain, to some extent, continues to act as if the limb were still there and connected to it through the nervous system.

Organizations are subject to their own version of the phantom-limb syndrome. Though customers' requirements and expectations change, the organization continues to respond to the old ones. When new data conflicts with time-honored organizational beliefs, the new data is rejected. A classic example of this syndrome occurred at General Motors during the early 1980s and is recounted by Gregory H. Watson in his book *Strategic Benchmarking*. During that period, a number of GM executives felt the tides of commerce running against them for the first time. J. D. Power and Associates had published its first survey of quality and customer satisfaction for the auto industry, and Japanese competitors dominated the top rankings. Power's survey was confirmed by GM's own customer-satisfaction data. In addition, two newly introduced auto platforms, the X- and J- cars, had been plagued by mechanical and assembly problems. There was even evidence that certain quality and performance tests of the J-car had been fudged to keep its development on schedule. The concerns of these executives, however, found no favor with GM's CEO, who, according to Watson, "professed disbelief and remained solid in his conviction that GM was the largest and finest manufacturing company in the world, the corporation against which others measured their own manufacturing quality competencies."[1]

Only time and a growing body of irrefutable evidence convinced GM's top executives that the phantom limb was really gone—that customer expectations and public perception of the company's products had indeed dramatically changed.

We encounter this type of pathology in many companies, and it is due to the fact that people are not perfectly rational. When confronted with facts that conflict with what they expect or desire, people find ways to negate, reinterpret, or discount those facts. The misalignment associated with this pathology is generally found in the company's processes. The company might have a great strategy and total buy-in from well-trained employees, but if they are responding to signals from a phantom limb, they will not develop or deliver what the market requires.

The antidote to the phantom-limb syndrome is a measurement system that people believe in. If employees have faith that the signals they're getting from customers and their competitors are relevant and accurate, they will be less inclined to deny the data and will stop responding to phantom signals.

Pathology 4: The Forked-Tongue Syndrome

Several years ago, analysts at a cellular-phone company we worked with made an important discovery: getting new customers on-line quickly had a big impact on customer retention. In other words, shortening the time between when new customers signed onto the service and when they could actually begin using the cell-phone made a difference in how long they would remain customers. The company's management was delighted with the finding since it pointed to a way of reducing customer churn rate, which all recognized as a major drag on revenue and profits. Wisely, they adopted rapid hookup as part of their strategy for expanding their customer base.

Rapid hookup, however, was more easily desired than delivered since it required process alterations involving both time and money. But no allowance for either of these changes had been made by corporate strategists. Strategy and operations had not been aligned. Appeals by regional units of the company for resources to make the necessary process changes were dismissed as just so much whining.

Does this sound familiar?

The forked-tongue syndrome exists when a company says one thing but acts in some contradictory way. It asks people to work as team players, yet rewards them for individual accomplishment. In the above case, the phone company mandated rapid hookup but refused to provide the resources to make it possible. The cure for this misalignment pathology is to coordinate strategy with the development of processes. The burden here is on those who propose changes in strategy. They need to apply systems thinking to strategy development—to say to themselves "If I change this, what else will have to be changed, and how feasible are those changes?"

In the cellular-phone case, certain operational processes needed to be changed. The strategists lacked the knowledge to identify the process changes, but, had they involved the appropriate employees in strategy formulation, this would not have been a problem.

Pathology 5: Market Myopia

This is a rare pathology, but one that can ruin an otherwise successful organization. In fact, success itself is often the incubator for its development.

Have you ever seen a company that has defined and identified its customer base with great accuracy, that understands its customers in detail, and that is dedicated to improving its ability to design and deliver products for those customers? If you make a list of companies like this, you'll notice that they are either among the current "best" or "former best" (and possibly defunct). Consider USAA, a company that specializes in providing insurance and other financial services to active and retired U.S. military officers and their dependents. By just about any definition, this is a *great* company—one of the best. It understands its targeted customer base like no other in its industry. Its processes for anticipating and delivering value to its customers are world-class and the envy of its competitors.

Unfortunately, the size of USAA's chosen market is not expanding, and forecasted reductions in the size of the U.S. military establishment only point to long-term contraction. The company has managed to grow, nevertheless, by expanding its set of products and services to credit cards, banking, investing, and travel services. But the concept of "share of wallet" can be taken only so far, and, in the absence of a change in strategy, we'd expect that USAA would have to work harder and harder to eke out future growth.

But this is a smart and well-managed company. It already recognizes this challenge and will probably adapt its strategy to the changing customer environment. Other companies are so myopic that they simply evaporate with their customer base.

Market myopia is a symptom of strategic failure. More often than not, it occurs when top managers fail to prepare their companies and their employees for market changes brought on by changing technology or regulation. When some steamrolling technology appears in an industry, companies that don't get on board with the technology get flattened. Massachusetts Institute of Technology professor James M. Utterback has documented a number of cases in which highly successful companies (and entire industries) have simply evaporated because they failed to make the transition from one generation of technology to the next.[2]

One of Utterback's classic cases involves the ice companies of nineteenth-century New England. These enterprises created commercial empires stretching to such far-off places as New Orleans, Havana, Calcutta, and Singapore. They accomplished this through efficient processes for harvesting, storing, and shipping natural ice from freshwater ponds. The great ice companies had developed their markets extremely well. They also developed their infrastructure and processes to greater and greater perfection. Huge fortunes were made.

When machine-made ice first entered the market in the 1870s, the ice barons responded as one would expect: they worked myopically at improving their processes and reducing costs. There is no evidence that any adopted the new technology. Eventually, the cost-effectiveness of machine-made ice caught up to and then leapt ahead of harvested ice, and the great New England ice empire melted away.

Pathology 6: Dead Man Walking

In a recent movie, "Dead Man Walking," prison guards summoned all to respectful attention and silence whenever a death-row convict was about to make the one-way journey from his cell to the execution chamber. "Dead man walking," they would call out. Some companies are so hopelessly misaligned that we find ourselves compelled to shout out the same thing.

What do these companies look like? The general profile looks something like this: The company was once the powerhouse in its industry, but is now perceived as "tired." It is losing market and is under pressure to improve profits. It has hundreds if not thousands of products in its active catalog and on the warehouse shelves. Though few of these contribute much to revenue or profits, the company cannot bring itself to weed out the deadwood. Some product managers have vested interests in keeping these products going and, so, fight for their continuation. Others worry about plant overcapacity if the product line is contracted. Sales reps lobby for as many different products as possible.

Companies like this have generally lost touch with the larger environment of customers, technology, and competitors. For them, especially the large ones, they see *themselves* as the environment. Consider AT&T in the early postbreakup period. As far as its product engineers were concerned, AT&T had the best telephones possible. You could drop one of its phones out of a ten-story window or drive over it with a city bus and it would still work. "These are the best-quality phones in the world," they once told us. Typical of organizations that see themselves as *the world*, AT&T engineers in those days defined quality in terms of their own technical standards and specifications. Customers, who didn't worry about their telephones falling from tenth-floor windows, wanted something quite different. They wanted less-expensive phones in different colors and with many different features. They wanted quality defined in *their* terms.

Dead-man-walking firms are in a death spiral, having lost sight of the competitive environment as well as the concerns of their customers. To improve results, they work at reducing costs and becoming more and more cost-effective in producing, in fact, what fewer and fewer people want. They reduce outlays for Research and Development, locking themselves into existing products with little or no market appeal and eventually forcing themselves out of business.

WHAT SICK COMPANIES LOOK LIKE

Each of the pathologies just described has a particular shape in terms of our alignment diagnostic tool, as shown in Figure 3-2. If you are curious about how your organization shapes up against our tool, you can do your own diagnosis using the blank diagnostic form that is found in Appendix 1.

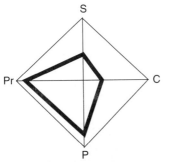

Tyranny of One

Process improvement activities are failing to meet customer needs because there is poor cross-functional integration around the customer's voice.

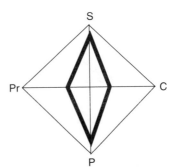

Strategy Interruptus

Strategy hasn't been effectively deployed and, so, goes nowhere. There is no passion or commitment.

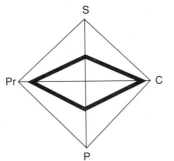

The Phantom-Limb Syndrome

People work hard to satisfy customer needs that no longer exist. The company drives into the future with its eyes on the rearview mirror.

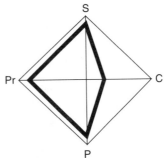

Forked-Tongue Syndrome

Strategy may be okay, but deployment is plagued by mixed signals from the top.

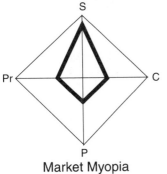

Market Myopia

People and processes are focused on current customers, but the larger strategy is out of touch with the competitive environment.

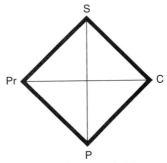

Dead Man Walking

Living in the past. Not clear on the customers to please or the processes to fix. Strategy and people are totally disconnected.

Figure 3-2. A typology of alignment pathologies.

Pathologies that Cause Misalignment

1. *Tyranny of One:* Exists in companies whose employees don't understand their contribution to the customer. It occurs when individuals and departments fail to communicate across the company and to connect with the customer. Although departments do a good job individually, they have little or no impact on their customers' satisfaction.

2. *Strategy Interruptus:* Experienced by companies that develop good strategies, but fail to implement them. Strategy interruptus happens when the strategy is developed without the involvement of those individuals responsible for its implementation.

3. *The Phantom-Limb Syndrome:* When companies fail to recognize changing customer requirements and new competitors, and continue to respond to old signals, they are responding to a phantom limb. This pathology persists as people find ways to negate, reinterpret, or discount data that conflict with their own expectations.

4. *The Forked-Tongue Syndrome:* When companies say one thing but act in a contradictory way, they're suffering from the forked-tongue syndrome. This syndrome occurs when the people making strategic changes within the company fail to take process changes into account and therefore do not support them or the people attempting to execute the new strategy.

5. *Market Myopia:* Exists in highly successful companies that fail to change their business strat-

(Continued)

(Continued)

egy to meet changes in the marketplace. Market myopia occurs when top managers fail to prepare their companies and their employees for market changes brought on by advancing technology or new regulations.

6. *Dead Man Walking:* Experienced by companies that are hopelessly misaligned. Once industry powerhouses, these organizations are crumbling under their own weight. A company that loses touch with its customers, competitors, and business environment because its sees *itself* as the environment is a dead man walking.

SO WHAT'S THE CURE?

Diagnosis gets us past the visible symptoms of organizational misalignment to their root causes. But having found the cause, what's the cure? The cure is to achieve vertical and horizontal alignment. Chapters 4, 5, and 6 provide a proven framework as well as techniques for doing this. In these we'll explain

1. How you can deploy strategy rapidly through your organization while creating higher levels of performance,

2. How processes can be better aligned with what customers want and need, and

3. How managers can create accurate and useful indicators for *staying* aligned.

4

Aligning Activities with Intentions: Vertical Alignment

Vertical alignment is about rapidly moving the company strategy through the organization, turning intentions into actual work. It gets strategy down to the ground where it can do some good. For many organizations, strategy never fully diffuses through the company—it is never completely *deployed.* It ends up in high-minded conversations between senior managers and in dusty binders that few bother to read. But aligned organizations are invigorated by strategy; it pulses from top to bottom. For them, it is a force that directs and energizes everyone and the work they do.

What accounts for the difference between these two kinds of organizations? In our experience, the difference is in how strategy is created and how people are engaged with it. When strategy is *created with the involvement of employees and customers and deployed rapidly and well,* it releases the untapped energy of employees and aligns activities with intentions.

A hierarchy that stresses command and control can claim to do neither. The reason is that most work today takes place in widely dispersed departments and business units that are far from the levers of control. Information and power have migrated to these outer edges. Whether it is shop floor employees making decisions about how best to attach the rear bumper to an automobile, or a telephone service representative engaged in face-to-face transactions with customers, sensing and responding to the marketplace takes place at the edges of the organization, not at the top.

> Strategy that reflects the contributions of the workforce and is executed rapidly and effectively will 1) align activities with the intentions of the business and 2) invigorate employees.

Attempts to create and effect strategy from the top are too slow and out of touch with markets and with the people who must execute the company's game plan. Citizens Utilities' Daryl Ferguson acknowledged as much when he told us his company was investing heavily in one of its business units because "the people in the front lines are telling us that the market's there, and the customers are telling us they like our service. . . . We would not be making this change without feedback from the bottom up and the customer."

When employees at the edges are authorized to act—as many are today—you'd better be sure that they understand and support the plan. Individual ownership and personal responsibility on the part of the employee (or empowerment, to quote popular business speak) is necessary to get things done right.

But empowerment without alignment is a recipe for disaster. In the absence of alignment, strategy can be interpreted differently by different people. Like the game "telephone," clear directives may emanate from the top, but they are inevitably twisted or reinterpreted as they pass from person to person. The result? Different parts of the organization career off in separate directions, and the power and energy of the business are dissipated.

Vertical alignment is a challenge for every company as it becomes larger and more geographically distributed. Getting everyone to sing from the same songbook becomes more and more difficult. FedEx went from being a small operation with a handful of employees and facilities in the 1970s to an organization of more than 120,000 employees in facilities scattered around the world. Its many different and distributed activities needed to be aligned with the company's key objectives. Says Fred Smith, "When you're small you can tie those things together at a more simplistic level—by culture, or philosophy, or guiding principles. But as things get bigger and more complex, they have to be welded together through mathematical indices."

Measurement is key to achieving vertical alignment.

The concept of integrating or aligning a company through measurement is akin to the Baldrige Award's methodology of using measurement to align key systems and processes. Measurement is one of several keys to vertical alignment. Performance measures tell employees the extent to which they are achieving goals in key areas, such as quality and customer service. When rewards and recognition are tied to these same measures, people are inclined to stay focused on the goals that management is trying to accomplish. A commonality of interests exists throughout the organization. The vice presidents of human resources for three Baldridge Award-winning companies affirmed this proposition. In fact, they recommend making performance measures and rewards the starting point in preparing for the Baldrige examination.

But what to measure? To be useful, measures must be tied to key company objectives—what we earlier described as the main thing. FedEx's main thing is absolutely reliable express delivery and a complete and accurate record at the end of every transaction. For FedEx to meet this objective, every employee must understand it: not just Smith and his top managers, but each of its 120,000+ employees worldwide. FedEx accomplishes this by a corporate philosophy, a set of key corporate goals, and measurement systems that track how well the company is delivering on its express mission. "Everybody who works here understands implicitly the parameters within which they operate," says Smith. "Everybody's goals, every year, are somehow related back to the business mission." Indeed, the company is systematic in tying every employee to a people goal, a service goal, and a profit goal. This measurement system is clear, public, and easily understood—and it aligns work with the purpose of the business.

The strategy deployment process at AirTouch focuses all employees on three to six key corporate goals that relate to the corporate mission. Lee Cox states, "It's like ants in the forest that are going to move a big tree. You might say, 'how are they going to do that?' They will eventually. Everybody knows exactly which piece they're going to go after, and how it relates to the other pieces."

> Measures must be tied to your main thing in order to align how you work with the purpose of the business.

PDR: A Framework for Achieving Vertical Alignment

To deploy strategy rapidly and effectively from top to bottom, we recommend a framework called PDR, an ongoing cycle of planning, deployment, and review (Figure 4-1). This cycle should occur in every business unit and at every level. In our experience, this cycle of activities allows even large organizations to successfully crystallize strategy and get it into play in 60 to 90 days. To readers whose companies drag out strategic planning alone for one or two years—to say nothing of implementation—this may seem incredible. But we've seen it happen.

Since we first began using PDR in 1993, it has helped companies confused by their changing business environments and failing to move forward. Many of these companies were hopelessly bogged down in strategic planning that never seemed to get finished. Others could not get action on the plans they had.

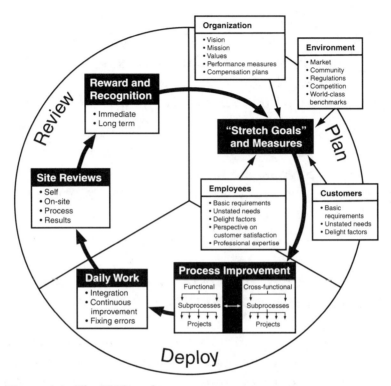

Figure 4-1. The PDR cycle.

PDR helped these companies to focus thought and energy on the critical aspects of the business. Once they did this, they briskly moved forward. They were vertically aligned.

Let's consider PDR—one letter at a time.

PLANNING: HOW THE MAIN THING BECOMES THE MAIN EVENT

Every business makes plans: strategic plans, annual business plans, business unit plans. Traditional plans emerge from a small number of people at or near the top and are expressed in financial and budgetary terms. The planning needed to achieve the vertical alignment that is advocated here is much different. It emerges from a process that involves the people at the top, who must then lead the much larger body of people needed to translate plans into real work.

PDR planning begins with the main thing of the organization. For PDR purposes, the main thing might be either the highest level purpose of the organization or the single most important thing that will improve performance in the near term. For a prison system we worked with, for example, the main thing was to become the "supplier of choice." That might seem odd for a prison system, but this particular one was faced with privatization, and it wanted to be seen as the superior supplier of prison services. For one division of a communications company, the main thing was growth. For a certain chemical company, earnings before interest and taxes (EBIT) was the main thing. Whatever it is, the main thing must be something determined by customers. And planning must be driven by customer values, not by dollar values.

Steps for Identifying Your Main Thing

To determine the main thing for any given unit, we suggest you do the following:

1. Bring together the people who represent the different perspectives on which you intend to focus.

(Continued)

(*Continued*)

2. Conduct dialogue on what is important to the business; make sure that each perspective has a voice.

3. Simplify the choices that emerge from dialogue, but stay loose, and allow for many ways to contribute.

4. Select the choice that creates passion and is consistent with organizational strategy.

PDR Deliverables

There is much more to effective planning than just identifying your main thing. Effective planning demands a coordinated set of critical success indicators, stretch goals, and activities and tactics. These are the "deliverables" of PDR planning. The structure tree in Figure 4-2 demonstrates how these planning elements fit together, matching intentions and activities with the main thing.

> Effective planning is driven by your main thing and demands a set of critical success indicators, stretch goals, and activities and tactics.

Here's an example of how the structure tree works. If the main thing was to expand the customer base, several critical success indicators might be associated with that effort: average account longevity, rate of new accounts per month, or other quantitative measures. To boost performance, management would attach a

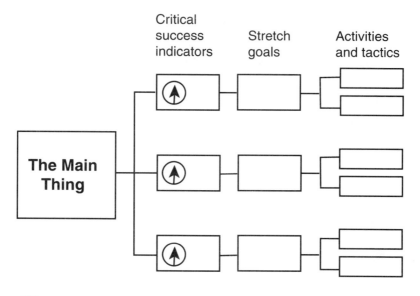

= a quantitative measure

Figure 4-2. The planning structure tree.

stretch goal to each. A stretch goal is a very ambitious, highly targeted opportunity for breakthrough improvements in performance. For account longevity, for instance, a stretch goal might be to increase average account longevity by 50 percent in two years. Managers and employees charged with that goal would then determine which activities and tactics had the greatest effect on account longevity and find ways to improve or redesign them.

Because they are so fundamental to organizational performance, PDR planning goals should take several years to achieve. To effect behavior, however, they must have intermediate stages. If, for example, a five-year goal is to reduce facility downtime to zero, there should be annual goals, each bringing this larger goal closer to reality. Thus, the first year's goal might be to train all line workers in both preventive maintenance and equipment repair. The goals for years two and three respectively might be to design and then build a backup production system that includes replacement parts and equipment.

Goals Must Make People Stretch

Stretch goals are ambitious, highly targeted opportunities for breakthrough improvements in performance. Many of our greatest business leaders have used them to transform their companies. When he was CEO of Hewlett-Packard, John Young used stretch goals to ratchet up the performance of the entire corporation. Every few years he would articulate a stretch goal that was demanding, important, and clearly stated. For example, during the late 1970s, HP data indicated warranty failure rates of about two percent per year, not a bad measure of product reliability for an American firm at the time. But they were not good enough for Young or for HP. So in 1980, Young announced that the firm would aim for a tenfold decrease in the failure rate of HP hardware products. Six years later, frustrated by the time it took his company to get new products into the market, Young announced a new corporate-wide stretch goal: cut time-to-market in half. In both cases, employees rose to the challenge and met Young's demanding goals.*

General Electric's Jack Welch is another successful practitioner of stretch goals. Like Young's,

(Continued)

(Continued)

his are demanding, important, and clear to all: "First, Second, or Out," a goal that every GE operating unit would be first or second in its markets within three years or be sold; and "Six Sigma," a corporate-wide initiative adopted in 1996 to improve quality and slash the costs associated with quality problems.†*

---

*Frank, Gertz, and Porcher, "Leader For Growth," *Strategy and Leadership* 24, no. 5 (Sept-Oct 1996), 10.

†As described by Gregory Watson, who worked at HP at the time, "In true Youngean style, he did not proclaim any method for achieving that goal; his managers were left to figure out how to do it." See Gregory H. Watson, *Strategic Benchmarking* (New York: John Wiley & Sons, 1993), 96.

In a full-blown PDR exercise, every level, every department, and every unit of the enterprise has its own structure tree, which is linked to the appropriate higher-level unit (shown in Figure 4-3). Here, a stretch goal for one unit might become the main thing for the next lower-level unit. An activity or tactic of that unit might logically be the main thing for the next lower unit, and so forth. This system of linked structure trees gives every unit and every employee a set of goals and measures that contribute to the main thing of the business.

We recently worked with a Malaysian conglomerate to link its operating units through a planning system like the one just described. We began the PDR process with a three-day workshop that included the chairman and the presidents of the operating companies. The presidents then repeated the PDR process for their

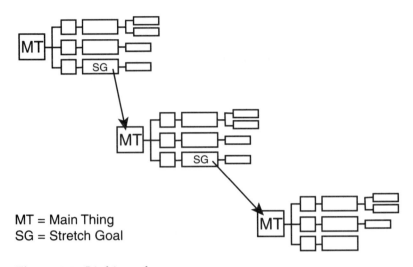

MT = Main Thing
SG = Stretch Goal

Figure 4-3. Linking of structure trees.

companies and insisted that each functional area within those companies do the same. Ultimately, each of the operating companies aligned itself in support of the conglomerate's strategy, and each aligned its internal activities with its own strategic goals.

A well-earned celebration dinner was served at the end of the three-day marathon. The group's chief financial officer told us a story. It went something like this:

According to old Chinese legend, there was once a Mongolian prince who begged his father for the chance to prove his worth in battle. The father honored his son's request and granted him 1,000 warriors. The prince assembled his horsemen, erected a large target for them to shoot at, and gave the command to shoot. A thousand arrows flew through the air—some hit the target, most did not. Each day the prince drilled the warriors, making the target smaller and smaller as accuracy increased. The final test of the warriors' readiness was to have them shoot at a horse. Now, Mongolian horsemen prized their animals more than anything else on earth. Yet, at the prince's command, 1,000 arrows were unleashed and 1,000 arrows hit their mark. "Now we are ready!" the prince declared. That prince, our colleague told us, was Genghis Khan—the infamous warrior and leader who went on to conquer territory 500 times larger than his own.

The CFO turned to the chairman, raised his glass, and said, "Now we are ready as well!"

Citizens Utilities

For a simplified picture of how structure trees work in planning, consider this abridged version used several years ago at the executive level of Citizens Utilities, a $1.3 billion company with 60 operating units. (For a more complete description of how Citizens linked structure trees to deploy strategy, see Appendix 2.) This company determined that its main thing would be to establish itself as the employer and supplier of choice. This goal was strategic, in that customer and employee surveys conducted in mid-1991 revealed truly disturbing information. Rate payers knew little about what the company was doing, and what they did know they didn't like. Given a choice, 43 percent of these customers would take their business elsewhere. Employees were equally negative about the company. In their view, Citizens Utilities did not provide good service, didn't care about its customers, and was not an organization for which they enjoyed working. To become the employer and supplier of choice, the company developed subgoals and success indicators for each. What "employer of choice" and "supplier of choice" meant were defined and measured through various indexes (Figure 4-4).

Daryl Ferguson has aligned his entire organization around financial, customer, and employee goals, and instituted a rigorous review process that he personally conducts. Citizens has surpassed its 1996 goals in each of these areas. He was pleased to tell us, "We just got a study from the Yankee Group that compared us to all the regional Bells, and we lead in local service in almost every category."

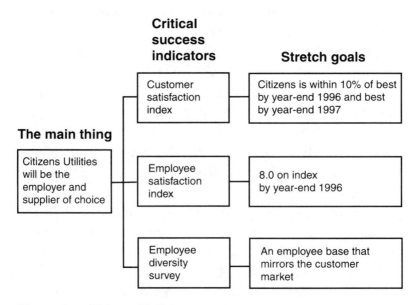

Figure 4-4. Citizens Utilities structure tree.

Creating Stretch Goals

Peter Drucker once said that concentration is the key to economic results. That's valuable advice when you're creating goals. Stretch goals should be few—three to five—since organizations cannot successfully pursue more than that at one time. If you try to bite off too many initiatives at one time, your efforts will become diluted and unmanageable.

The planning phase of PDR identifies the main thing and a few critical stretch goals. The goals are best determined by listening intently to four "voices."

- *The Voice of the Customer:* Organizations that do not listen to changing customer requirements are left behind by competitors that do. Indeed, a core competency of any successful business is its ability to gather actionable data from customers. Sometimes feedback is indirect and inexplicit—the Japanese call such nuances *guzu-guzu,* or customer rumblings.
- *The Voice of the Organization:* A clear understanding of organizational mission, values, performance measures, and the knowledge that senior management has of the business.
- *The Voice of the Environment:* Every organization we work with is subjected to relentless and often pernicious change. Therefore, goals need to be fashioned that reflect a clear understanding of changing environmental

(Continued)

(Continued)
    forces such as competition, regulation, and technology.

- *The Voice of the Employee:* Employees are often overlooked as strategy is developed. Ultimately it's the employees who execute the strategy. The extent to which they are involved in the planning process often determines their willingness and ability to carry it out.

Enrichment and Commitment

The planning structure we have just described is mechanically sound. On paper, it works just fine. But does it work in the real world? The answer is yes *if* two conditions are met: 1) Strategy has been enriched by people in relevant parts of the organization, and 2) the people charged with implementing strategy are committed to it.

Enrichment is a consequence of active sharing. Good strategy is the product of great strategic thinkers. But *great* strategy is the product of many good thinkers sharing their ideas. The environment of modern business is simply too distributed and too complex for any individual or team of strategic planners to fully understand. This is why the insights of many thoughtful employees must be brought to bear on strategic issues.

Vincent P. Barabba has demonstrated the power of collaborative strategy making at General Motors. There, a new decision-making process has resulted in hybrid strategy alternatives far superior to those proposed initially. These hybrids contain the best elements of the several alternatives.[1] The GM method, which Barabba calls the "dialogue decision process," creates an environment of objectivity in which strategic alternatives are shared and rationally analyzed. This environment allows many people representing many different job functions to enrich existing alternatives or develop better ones.

> Great strategy is the product of *enrichment*, where many good thinkers come together and share ideas.

Commitment is the second element of effective strategic goals and a precondition for their successful deployment. It is a fact of human nature that people tend to support what they have created and tend not to support imposed programs. As a result, how we create strategy has a tremendous impact on the support it receives. People will trust a strategy only if they understand how it was created.

We advocate a three-step process for enlisting that trust:

1. Reveal the assumptions behind the strategy;

2. Describe the likely scenarios that emerge from the assumptions;

3. Explain the criteria for selecting one particular scenario and strategy over others.

> Like enrichment, commitment is developed through employee participation.

Zytech, Inc., a winner of the 1991 Baldrige Award, opens strategy planning to everyone, from janitors on up. This is not to advocate "democratizing" the process of developing strategic goals. Given the opportunity, many individuals and business units will lobby for goals that interest them with little thought to the interests of customers or other stakeholders. To avoid such a myopic response, managers need to seek employee feedback to strategies that emerge from market data through a procedure such as catchball, described below. The point of sharing the strategies is to elicit ideas for improvement, identify pitfalls, and get a "reality check" from the people closest to the action.

Enrich your strategy with ideas that come from the link between the marketplace and the company—your employees.

Playing Catchball

One proven method for assuring both enrichment and commitment is the Japanese technique of "catchball." Catchball involves many levels of the organization and is used to improve strategic goals and initiatives. It facilitates the exchange of information and feedback about a strategy or plan with those directly affected by it. When properly played, it is a freewheeling exercise in which strategic priorities and people's ideas for achieving them pass rapidly around the organization, crossing functional lines. In the process, plans are enriched by the insights of many players. And, by allowing everyone to help shape the organization's future, high levels of commitment and motivation are achieved.

The catchball process helps organizations avoid several familiar problems:

- Strategy that is owned by the top but ignored by everyone else
- Good employees who fail to focus on key goals
- Lack of commitment and momentum in the company

To make catchball work, senior managers circulate through the organization, engaging middle managers and employees in the "game." The rules of the game are simple. First comes the "toss"—a senior manager throws out an idea for consideration, perhaps his or her version of a strategic goal. Someone must "catch" the idea—that is, take the trouble to understand it and reflect on it. Then, anyone with a suggestion for improving the first idea can make the next toss in the form of an enhanced iteration of the original idea. Others then catch, reflect upon, and improve the idea. This process isn't as simple as it sounds. The idea catcher must be sufficiently open-minded to consider the idea fairly before reacting. For many people, this is almost an unnatural act. The catchball cycle is repeated, as in Figure 4-5, until the idea is either fully developed or abandoned.

If you are a senior manager, we can almost guarantee that playing this game with an open mind will result in ideas that are superior to any you personally had or expected to find. And you will find them faster. Catchball or a similar technique will quickly enrich your strategy with ideas that come directly from the link between the marketplace and the company. It is from this link, in fact, that much of today's best business strategy is developed.

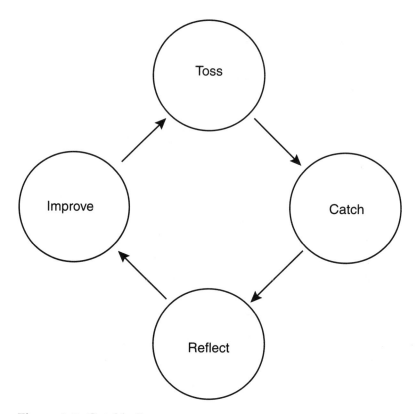

Figure 4-5. Catchball.

DEPLOYMENT: GETTING STRATEGY DOWN TO THE GROUND

Strategy is often like desert rain. Before the raindrops hit the desert floor, they evaporate, creating little or no effect below. In business, deployment is what gets strategy down to the ground where it can do some good. It is the action- and people-oriented part of PDR.

Well-deployed business strategy is evident in the behavior of people at work. They are busy doing what management expects them to do, and they are doing what they know to be important and in their interest to do.

> Deployment gets strategy down to the ground.

The seeds of successful deployment are planted back in the planning phase. When management involves its people in the development of strategy—through catchball or some other means—it has already developed the understanding and commitment required for successful deployment. Employees are prepared to understand the *what* of strategic goals, and managers and supervisors have to make the *what* explicit. But employees must also understand the *why* and the *how*. One of our long-term clients, Jet Propulsion Laboratory (JPL) provides a good example of how management can help employees understand the what, the why, and the how of strategic goals.

Understanding the "What"

Jet Propulsion Laboratory had every incentive to change the way it was doing business. Its costs and processes were out of control, and it was depending on out-of-date technology. The world of space exploration and funding was changing, and JPL had to change with it. The days of the big, 15-year, megabillion dollar projects were over.

The company responded by developing a new set of strategic goals designed around new customer requirements for quicker, cheaper, and more frequent unmanned space exploration. Senior managers shared these goals through a series of voluntary meetings that attracted 1,200 of the organization's 6,500 employees. At each of these meetings, every senior manager was responsible for talking about one of 10 strategies. After each presentation, employees were asked, "What did you hear?" This question led to dialogue in which employees discussed the strategies, internalized them, and reached greater clarity about the *what*. This prepared the group to tackle the next question—*why*.

Why Should I?

Next, JPL senior managers asked people to answer the question, "*Why* are these strategies important to me?" For alignment to work, employees must see clear and important personal benefits in supporting a strategy. These can be compensation, more challenging work, an opportunity to influence, even company survival and job security! If dialogue reveals that not all affected employees can identify a clear stake in the strategy and its success, then management must rethink its system of rewards and recognition.

How Should We Work

Finally, JPL managers asked, "Now, *how* do we need to work differently to accomplish our strategic goals?" Working differently means redesigning and/or improving the processes that deliver goods and services. For instance, in an environment of quicker, cheaper space projects, JPL employees had to develop the ability to quickly move technical specialists around the organization from project to project. This was anathema in the old environment, where project managers "hoarded" people with particular skills. Changing the environment required a new information system that would indicate who had skills and knowledge and where they were located. It also required a willingness to share resources.

At the Tenth NASA Continual Improvement and Reinvention Conference, Daniel Goldin, the administrator of NASA, captured everyone's attention when he told the audience that he was prepared to shut JPL down when he took over NASA. He felt they were intellectually arrogant and building "technological dinosaurs." He went on to add, however, that in the preceding three years the transformation at the lab "has been stunning." He now had every confidence in the ability of Jet Propulsion Laboratory to fulfill its new mission. His confidence is well placed as the lab demonstrated its ability to rapidly and effectively respond to its new operating reality.

Process-Activated Training

Working differently also means learning to work more effectively. One way of doing that is through a training system called PATS (Process Activated Training System). Developed by our colleague Dr. Don Fisher, executive director of the Mid-South Quality and Productivity Center, PATS identifies experts in different subject matter throughout the organization who understand the strategy. It then creates a system in which others learn from the experts. With PATS, the people who are most skillful and most aligned teach each other how to improve and make the strategy work.

Subject-matter experts in PATS are individuals who have mastered a particular subprocess, for example, putting on a door at Volvo Trucks or stocking shelves at Wal-Mart. According to Fisher, 10 percent of a company's workforce eventually become subject-matter experts, who then form a network for spreading continuous improvement throughout the organization. These experts pass on their know-how to peers through a process that is mapped and tracked by a Lotus Notes–based system. The benefits of this system include dramatic reductions in training time, increased productivity, higher morale, and real worker empowerment.

PATS helps companies align themselves vertically by enabling employees to realize company goals on their own. According to Fisher, employees "define what best practices are in their own work areas and what are the best steps to take to complete these processes. The system is employee-driven, not management-driven."

Guidelines for Deploying Your Strategy

- Organize voluntary meetings at which you explain the strategy.
- Ask the three key questions:

  1. *What* is the strategy as you heard it?

  2. *Why* is it *personally* important to you?

  3. *How* do we need to work differently together?

  (Continued)

(Continued)
- Be a facilitator of dialogue. Get people to talk with each other about the strategy, not to you as the boss. But listen to what they're saying!
- Document key points made by participants and share them with others.
- Use the best suggestions as bases for process improvements.

Warp Speed Ahead!

Getting strategy right, and getting it down to the rank and file, is obviously important. The need to do it *fast* is just as important.

We learned this the hard way. Years ago, when we began consulting on quality deployment, we always started with the small executive group at the top. After a week or so of working with them, we would hold a similar but larger session with the next tier of managers. And so on and so on until, months later, all affected groups had been informed and coached on quality deployment. Everything would now be ready to go. But by then, some of the energy and commitment of the earlier groups had dissipated. Some managers would have turned their attention to other problems, and the guardians of the status quo would have had time to circle the wagons against change.

Worse still, the fast pace of contemporary business requires frequent shifts in strategy. If deployment cannot keep pace, the organization will be launching a new strategy before the old one is fully deployed.

To cope with these problems, our current deployment sessions bring together many more people representing many units or levels simultaneously. At a recent project done for the Government Accounting Office, our deployment session was attended by 65 managers representing four different levels. At another, over 700 people participated at one time.

REVIEW, REVIEW, REVIEW

The final step in PDR is review. Review is the little gear that makes the entire wheel turn. Here, senior managers watch for problems in strategic deployment on the front lines.

When a doctor reviews the progress of her hospitalized patients, she does not do so from the comfort of her office. She knows that there is no substitute for seeing and listening to patients, reading the intangible signs in their voices and faces. And for the patients themselves, a bedside visit from the doctor and words of concern and encouragement can be as therapeutic as any medicine.

Senior executives, too, must see and be seen. They must set aside their reports and observe the people

---

The review process helps senior executives monitor progress toward actualizing the company's strategy and assists middle managers and employees in refining their activities and energizing processes.

and activities that bring strategy to life. Seeing people at work and talking to front-line employees fills in the spaces that other information systems leave empty. Being seen in the workplace assures everyone that their work and the strategy are important.

We appreciated the power of the review process only after several visits to Japan. One company we visited, the Sanwa Bank, stands out. Each of its 231 branch managers is reviewed annually in the manager's own office by the bank chairman or one of his close associates. During these visits, the chairman asks 10 questions, which are known in advance. It's not a pop quiz. Included are questions about the strategic goals of the bank and how the manager's branch fits in. Pity the manager who is not prepared. Failure to satisfy the chairman on any of his questions results in what the Japanese refer to as a "career terminating event."

The review process is meant to monitor progress toward stretch goals, help middle managers and employees make midcourse adjustments, and energize process improvements. One way to do this is through a series of formal questions. Executives should pick these questions carefully, because managers will use them as indicators of what executives really care about. As the old saying goes, "What interests my boss fascinates me."

Executives should ask managers the following questions:

- "What steps are you taking to promote communication and cooperation across functions?"

- "What progress have you made in reaching our stretch goals? What are the greatest obstacles?"
- "What data are you gathering from customers? Does it conflict with the assumptions of our strategy?"
- "What do you need from me to help you accomplish your goals?"

For non-managerial employees, executives should ask a slightly different set of questions:

- "Do you understand our strategy? How does what you're doing now fit in?"
- "What improvement initiatives are going on in your area right now?"
- "Are you recognized for what you do? What forms of recognition matter to you?"
- "What do you need to do your job better?"

The Importance of Reviews

Executives we've interviewed say that review is the most important part of strategy deployment. So they are diligent in reviewing people at all levels.

Daryl Ferguson of Citizens Utilities said, "I've done four president-level reviews, a headquarters staff review, and interviews with some 400 employees in small groups this year."

Lee Cox of AirTouch would remind his employees that "reviews are not about my company, but about their company. They own it and manage it. They're focused on the customer, the mar-

(Continued)

(*Continued*)

ket, and on our competitors. They're not doing all this to please me, but to satisfy themselves."

For an example of senior management review questions, consider those used by Jim Orr at UNUM, which are found in Appendix 3.

THE POWER OF VERTICAL ALIGNMENT

Vertical alignment appeals to most people's sense of logic. But so do many things that fail to hold up in practice. What about vertical alignment? Our experiences indicate that vertical alignment has value that can be measured in dollars and cents—and that's something everyone can relate to. Consider the case of the Earle M. Jorgensen company (EMJ).

For EMJ, the country's largest independent steel and materials distributor, aligning employees to the company's strategy has been the key to turning this tradition-bound company into a nimble, new competitor. Since merging with competitor Kilsby-Roberts in 1990, the company has grown into a $1 billion juggernaut and has earned accolades for its managerial excellence.

According to Chairman Neven Hulsey, the turn-around began soon after Hulsey, then CEO of Kilsby-Roberts, teamed with top managers to merge with EMJ in a leveraged buyout. This move came just as profound changes were reshaping the industry. More distributors were vying for the same customer base, global competition was increasing, and customers were demanding lower prices and higher quality. As a result, EMJ and other leading distributors were forced to change from their traditional roles as passive materials suppliers, who warehoused and shipped materials, to being value-adding partners, who processed materials and cut customer costs by storing and delivering materials in a just-in-time manner. "We had to prove our worth at managing the process, not just selling metals," said Hulsey.

This radical shift in strategy required a massive cultural transformation. Once a heavily bureaucratic and hierarchical organization, EMJ had to empower its employees to think on their own and make rapid decisions in the areas they knew best.

With the help of our consulting firm, Organizational Dynamics, Inc. (ODI), EMJ embarked on an ambitious program of transforming its culture to enable it to implement its evolving strategy. Realizing that success depended on the understanding and cooperation of everyone in the organization, management implemented an ambitious program of educating employees about the change process. They were careful to conduct this training as listeners and coaches.

EMJ used PDR in key areas such as process improvement, cycle-time reduction, and customer satisfaction. For EMJ, the PDR process created a shared understanding of the company's mission among employees. Starting from the top and then moving through the company, these cascading PDRs taught groups of employees, who in turn educated others, about where EMJ was going and how they personally fit in.

PDR helped the company to make the transition from merely supplying steel and materials to completely managing that function for its customers. This reinvention enabled the company to redefine its role for customers. With Halliburton Energy Services, for instance, EMJ went from being an outside materials supplier to an active participant in Halliburton's internal processes, assuming management of their materials. EMJ set up shop within Halliburton facilities and managed to decrease the number of its global suppliers from over 100 to 3.

Inventory is key to EMJ's business, since inventory and receivables represent two-thirds of the company's assets. "When you talk about inventory, people have to understand that it's not inventory reduction, it's inventory management," said vice president Randy Haas. Since the buyout, the company has introduced a key measure to its employees: ROSI, or return of stock inventory. ROSI tracks the relationship of inventory to gross profit. At a ROSI of 1.0, the company is earning one dollar of gross profit for every dollar of inventory.

EMJ set a goal of increasing its ROSI as part of the turnaround effort. The company implemented inventory quality action teams (QATs) to discuss ways to improve this number. The role of managers in these meetings was not to tell people what to do but, in the words of Neven Hulsey, to "sit there as an observer and make sure the conversation is going in the direction it should go." Through these meetings, employees started finding new ways to manage inventory and become more creative in supply chain management. After three years, EMJ had cranked up its ROSI to 1.62 and was aiming for 2.00.

This performance has allowed EMJ to reposition itself from a mere seller of supplies to an active participant in the companies with which it forms alliances.

The EMJ story underscores the power of vertical alignment: organizations that are vertically aligned get results. If your company or department cannot get people engaged and motivated to accomplish important goals, the cycle of plan-deploy-review can help. In the next chapter, we'll see how businesses can align their day-to-day operations with the needs of customers.

5

Ships Passing in the Night: Getting to Horizontal Alignment

In a wonderful little book called *Longitude*, Dava Sobel tells the story of an eighteenth-century clock maker, John Harrison, and his quest for the solution to "the problem of longitude." Until Harrison's time, mariners were unable to determine their east-west position on the globe. As a result, they were literally lost at sea as soon as their ships sailed beyond sight of land. Countless vessels were either lost or wrecked on darkened shores because their captains were unable to determine precisely where they were. One such disaster, and the event that launched Harrison's efforts, occurred in October 1707 when a squadron of British ships under the command of Sir Clowdisley Shovell was wrecked, a loss of four vessels and the lives of over 2,000 seamen including Shovell. As Sobel tells the story, Shovell and his ships were returning from Gibraltar after skirmishing with French Mediterranean forces. Thinking his position to be safely west of Ile d'Ouessant, an island off the coast of

Brittany, he ordered the squadron to press sail into what he reckoned to be open seas. Bearing into the darkness of a stormy night, four of Shovell's five ships foundered onto the rocky shore of the Scilly Islands. It was one of the greatest disasters of British maritime history.[1]

Even in Shovell's time, any sailor worth his salt could estimate his latitude (north-south position) well enough by the height of the North Star by night and the height of the sun at midday. But longitude was a far tougher nut to crack, and a practical method for determining it had eluded the best minds of the maritime nations for centuries.

Today's organizational captains have navigational problems analogous to those of earlier mariners. Like latitude, some indicators of performance, such as financial measures, are easy to obtain. They give managers a partial picture of how well their organizations are performing, but indicate less about *where* they are headed, recalling the mariner's joke: "The good news is that we're making excellent time. The bad news is that we're hopelessly lost."

To navigate effectively, companies must master organizational longitude. The instrument for this mastery is horizontal alignment. Horizontal alignment is reached when the organization *connects* with customers.

HARDWIRING THE COMPANY TO THE CUSTOMER

Just as vertical alignment ensures that company strategy is reflected in the behavior of every employee, horizontal alignment infuses the concerns of the customer into everything the organization does. Horizontal alignment links a company's actions with customer needs in ways that delight and create loyalty.

Horizontally aligned companies are easy to identify. They are so "hardwired" to customer requirements that the needs of their customers resonate with personnel and influence the company's strategy, processes, and behavior (Figure 5-1). These companies

- Have clear and explicit methods for gathering market data and disseminating it through the organization
- Link customer needs to their core processes for delivering goods and services
- Base every improvement on changing customer requirements
- Use the customer as the ultimate arbiter of how well they are doing

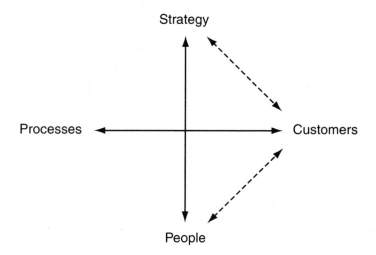

Figure 5-1. Horizontal alignment informs strategy and people.

Hallmark Cards, which holds a whopping 40 percent share of its multibillion-dollar industry, aligns itself to customer preferences and concerns like few others. It collects consumer preference data from its 9,000 independently owned card shops and mass-channel sales force. Its retail support center is in contact with customers 24 hours a day, every day. Consumer and store buyer data are actively distributed to Hallmark employees. It even brings card-store owners into its store design process.

Whirlpool Corporation, whose household appliances rate at or near the top of product quality ratings, is extremely committed to measuring, monitoring, and acting on customer satisfaction data. Its link to customers strengthened in 1994 when it implemented a system to monitor service performance down to the level of the individual employee.

CRI, a 1996 Baldrige Award winner in the small business category, is also this kind of company. It provides customized market research for its client. At the end of each project, its team members assess their own performance and at the same time survey the client on the quality, timeliness, and other aspects of the work. A bonus system rewards people for company, team, and individual performance; customer satisfaction counts for 20 percent of the award.

Rick Scott at Columbia provided us with perhaps our best example of horizontal alignment—of linking customer requirements with measurement and with process improvement. He said, "What we've done is determine what's important to our customers by talking to them continually, which then becomes our priority. . . . Then we create measurement systems, recognition systems, and reward systems that follow through on that." Columbia surveys 125,000 patients every quarter. Based on these data he believes that patients want four things:

1. *They want the best outcome they can get.* In our work with Columbia, we are helping to enhance and deploy a system that identifies best practices, whether clinical or administrative, and shares that information with every facility. Scott said, "We measure everything from the admitting process to the discharge process, to the response to the call button to what you thought of the food." They then rank order their facilities and acknowledge and reward the top 10 percent.

2. *They want to be treated with respect.* Scott said, "We'll give awards to the employees in the top 10 percent. All of these things, the recognition and measurement, create a very good alignment from the patients' point of view. Our primary customer is the patient. So we try to create recognition systems and reward systems. Our goal is that every employee gets this information and gets recognition."

3. *They want a reasonable price.* He said, "We measure how we can improve our costs, reduce our costs, so we can pass on better costs to the patient."

4. *They want to be treated with compassion.* He said, "We constantly highlight acts of compassion. We just came out with a small book written by our employees of examples, whether it's miracles or whether it's kindness. We highlight every example we can about what others in the company have done—works on the compassion side. . . ."

Columbia's focus on customer satisfaction and continuous quality improvement through the use of Best Practices has built a potent competitive force in health care. They have earned the respect of many within the field, including Dr. Dennis O'Leary. He told us:

> Some people have raised an eyebrow that Columbia has a very high rate of accreditation with commendation awards (top 10 percent). But Columbia has made quality one of its business strategies, and one of the possible implications of this is that people perhaps should be paying attention to what Columbia is doing right. I've been in some of these hospitals. The people who work in those hospitals know what is expected of them. They take a lot of pride in providing good care and good service to the people they serve. They believe that's how they're going to succeed tomorrow. It's not simply a matter of satisfying the Commission. It's having satisfied patients and families.

BE CUSTOMER FOCUSED OR DIE!

Just as mariners have learned to use the North Star to orient themselves to the earth's vertical axis, the organizational navigator must learn to take horizontal bearings from customers. The horizontally aligned company uses the customer voice both as a beacon and as a driver for the way individuals think, the way they work, and the way the organization is managed. Structure, decisions, and actions are based on what is best for the customer. The imperative to do so is compelling. As Jim Orr at UNUM says, "We've got to be customer focused, or we're going to die."

This is more easily said than done since, as a guide-post, customers present a number of serious challenges:

- Customer requirements change.
- The customer voice is often difficult to interpret.
- The customer voice speaks in the present tense, but companies must anticipate the future.
- Few employees of the typical organization have direct contact with customers.
- Understanding customers is rarely seen as a collective responsibility.

These difficulties can be overcome by the framework and techniques detailed in this chapter.

> Horizontally aligned companies use the customer voice as a beacon and a driver for the way the company thinks, works, and is managed.

So, What's New?

At this point, you may be asking: "What's new about being customer driven, customer oriented, or customer anything else?" Indeed, the "c" word has been a mantra for CEOs and management consultants for years. As early as 1960, Pillsbury president Robert Keith stated, "Soon it will be true that every activity of the corporation—from finance to sales to production—is aimed at satisfying the needs and desires of the consumer."[2]

We have come a long way in meeting Keith's expectation; no manager in our experience advocates simply building products and pushing them out the door. Still, being customer focused is more an ideal than a way of doing business for many companies. The problems of Sony Corporation during the late 1980s provides striking proof. For years, Sony led the world in consumer electronics, introducing new products that sparked the imagination of consumers around the world. So, a financial slump during the late 1980s baffled top management. What was wrong? Sony hadn't strayed from its strategy of rolling out innovative new iterations of successful products. On the contrary, it was deluging consumers with a wide range of choices for everything from video cameras to Walkman headphones. The problem was that the company was so focused on cycle time, cost reduction, and producing product derivatives that it took its eyes off the customers it expected would purchase its wizardry. Sony failed to ensure that it was producing what customers actually wanted. In fact, consumers were confused and overburdened by the cornucopia of products and product variations it churned out. Overwhelmed with product choice, many chose not to buy at all.[3]

Where TQM and Reengineering Fell Short

Both TQM and reengineering, two of the most widespread business improvement programs, take aim at the problem of customer focus. Indeed, both begin with the customer and work backwards, redesigning and/or improving every process in turn. Theoretically, this should align all horizontal activities in a tightly linked chain from supplier to company to customer.

Unfortunately, this hasn't happened. We know of dozens of TQM and reengineered companies that consistently miss delivery dates, fail to improve cycle time, or ignore customer requirements when they develop new products. Worse, they cannot seem to fix these problems. Most TQM and reengineering efforts have fallen short of horizontal alignment for two simple reasons. First, most TQM companies left the customer voice outside the processes of the organization (Figure 5-2). The job of listening to and interpreting that external voice fell to the small number of people with direct customer contact: sales and customer service personnel, and market researchers. Everyone else heard the customer voice either indirectly or not at all.

Second, in cases where TQM and reengineered *have* successfully brought the customer voice inside the company, that voice has been either ignored or

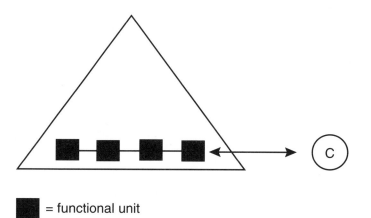

■ = functional unit

Figure 5-2. The voice of the customer left outside.

perceived differently by different functional groups, resulting in no shared understanding of what customers really want (Figure 5-3). No shared understanding of the customer that impacts company, its strategy, processes, or people.

Customer-related issues have held companies back from the full benefits of TQM and reengineering. Without a shared understanding of customers and their needs, different groups hear and interpret the customer's voice in ways that support what they are currently doing.

Despite investing in market research, many companies don't understand what customers want or what would delight them. The evidence for this is the huge percentage of new products and services that fail in the market. Most research never gets beneath the obvious to the root needs of customers. The result: they cannot anticipate what the customer will want in the future. FedEx anticipated customer needs with its highly successful package tracking system; no customer articulated this need to the company.

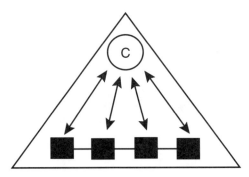

Figure 5-3. The voice of the customer is brought into the organization. But every function/group listens and draws its own conclusions.

Many suffer from what we call the "supplier mentality." A common symptom is a mismatch between supplier standards and customer requirements for the same item. For example, a major aerospace contractor produced a solar wind speed indicator for a space satellite that exceeded the customer's requirements by a factor of three times and also cost three times more. It was a marvel of engineering, but left the customer with a huge bill for capabilities it did not need.

Each of these problems is probably familiar to you. But how can you overcome them? In our experience, three things make it possible to improve alignment between your customers and the things you do as an organization: Answer the five key questions about what customers want and expect you to do; create a shared reality of customers and the competitive environment; and get to the customer's customer.

ANSWER THE FIVE BIG QUESTIONS

The *good* news is that we've reduced the many things you need to know about customers to a set of five fundamental questions:

1. What do our customers care about most?

2. What opportunities do we have to delight them?

3. How well are we satisfying our customers right now in terms of what they care about?

4. What are the "best-of-the-best" companies doing to delight their customers?

5. How does the way we operate now make us "difficult to do business with?"

Can you answer each of these questions? Can your boss or your direct reports? If you compared their answers, would they be the same?

U.S. businesses spend some $40 billion annually on market research, yet few companies can answer these fundamental questions with confidence. The problem is that most seek and acknowledge data that validates what they want to know about their own processes rather than what really delights customers.

Consider the typical hotel questionnaire. It asks 10 to 15 closed-ended questions, each designed to check the effectiveness of one or another of its existing processes: Was your bed made? Was the bathroom clean? Was a bar of soap in the dish? And so on. For frequent travelers who care about the quality of hotel accommodations, these questions address the *minimum* requirements for hotel quality. They make no effort to determine which of the hotel's amenities *really* matter to the traveler, or what new feature or amenity would earn the hotel the traveler's highest rating. Nor do they ask the million-dollar question: "What are other hotels doing that pleases you more?"

Contrast this with the Ritz-Carlton. Its questionnaires use open-ended questions to elicit meaningful guest feedback. And every time a guest books a room, the company adds to its customized guest database. Ritz-Carlton uses every transaction as an opportunity to better understand the customer: Do they want a feather or nonallergenic foam pillow? Do they prefer the *Wall Street Journal* or some other complimentary morning newspaper? Do they want an iron in the room? Accessible to every hotel in the Ritz-Carlton chain, this individualized guest history makes it possible for the company to anticipate its guest's preferences and has helped it earn one of the highest loyalty ratings in the services business.

The Two Toughest Questions

The toughest questions to answer of the five listed above are generally the first two:

1. What do our customers care about most?

2. What opportunities do we have to delight them?

As luck would have it, these are also the most important. These are the toughest questions because customers themselves have trouble answering them. What customers care about most and how we can delight them are usually informed by deep-seated or *root* needs that many customers cannot articulate. Discover these deep-seated needs and the game of business competition will be yours to lose.

What Do People Really Want?

Discovering customers' deep-seated needs is less daunting than business people generally suppose. It's true that many customers cannot articulate them on their own, but they can with a little help from what we call the "needs evolution technique." It helps companies do three things: identify unstated needs; translate these into *root needs,* which we define as "specific standards for delight"; and learn how these root needs can be met.

Here are the six steps you can use to discover your customers' root needs:

1. *Ask customers what they care about most in terms of your products and services and the way you provide them.* Most responses will be nonspecific: "I care about reliability." Get them to be more specific about what they mean, but don't lead them. For example, *don't* ask "When you say reliability are you talking about the expected life of the product or the warranty coverage?" Instead, say

"When you say reliability, what do you mean?"

"I mean that I can use the product for a long time with minimal serving."

"Anything else?"

"Yes, low repair costs."

"Anything else?"

Keep probing until the customer can give no further specifics.

2. *Ask customers to prioritize those "care-abouts."* Customers care about a lot of things, but some matter much more than others. You won't know which matter most unless you ask the question directly.

3. *Ask customers to define those care-abouts as specifically as possible.* Don't be reluctant to say "Please, tell me more."

4. *Continue these questions until the root needs are reached.* These tell you exactly what would satisfy a particular customer in the areas he or she cares about most. They also tell you how he or she would measure satisfaction in those areas.

5. *Ask customers to rank each root need.* Which is the most important of the indicated root needs? Now ask how well those needs are currently being satisfied.

6. *Identify opportunities for improvement.* Ask the customer how your current way of doing business gets in the way of delighting him or her. Find out what the best-of-the-best are doing to delight that customer.

Six Steps for Getting at Your Customers' Root Needs

1. Ask customers what they care about most in terms of your products and services and the way you provide them.

2. Ask customers to prioritize those "care-abouts."

3. Ask customers to define those care-abouts as specifically as possible.

4. Continue these questions until the root needs are reached.

5. Ask customers to rank each root need.

6. Identify opportunities for improvement.

Opportunities to Delight

To build and *keep* relationships with customers, you want to delight them in as many ways as possible. Opportunities to do this can occur in three phases of the relationship: *before* you deliver the goods, *during* delivery, and *after* the fact. Each phase contains two opportunities to delight: 1) you can ensure that the *products or services* meet or exceed customer needs, and 2) you can develop and maintain *trust*. The matrix in Figure 5-4 identifies the opportunities in each phase of the customer relationship.

Which opportunities is *your* organization taking to delight its customers?

Finding examples of customer delight is one of our easiest jobs, for a simple reason: Delighted customers enjoy telling you about their experience, and they won't shut up!

One of our colleagues has been a fan of Hewlett-Packard for over 10 years. If HP went into the breakfast

	Before	**During**	**After**
Products and Services	• Learn about the customer's situation • Verify the customer's needs • Align your capabilities to deliver	• Deliver expected outcomes plus extras • Verify satisfaction • Make adjustments to changing needs	• Seek immediate feedback • Verify performance • Recover instantly from problems
Trust	• Demonstrate experience • Agree on a working relationship • Show you care	• Demonstrate skills • Keep the customer informed • Treat the customer as special	• React positively to feedback • Apologize for any problems • Make a personal commitment to the customer

Figure 5-4. Opportunities to delight.

cereal business tomorrow, he'd be eating the stuff at every meal! An initial experience triggered his delight, and subsequent contacts with the company have sustained his satisfaction and loyalty. The experience that triggered his delight involved the company's repair of his old HP financial calculator back in the mid-1980s. Here's what happened. After four years of poking the keys and spilling coffee on this calculator, it developed one "sticky" function key. Our friend sent it off to the HP service center from which it was returned in perfect working order for a small service charge. This is what he expected. What *delighted* him was the handwritten note he received with his good-as-new calculator:

Dear Mr. X:

Instead of fixing the present value key on your calculator, I put in our newly designed key pad. It's much better than the original and should prevent your other keys from developing the same problem. Hope you like it. No extra charge.

That "no extra charge" probably cost Hewlett-Packard a grand total of fifty cents, but it was a great investment. Our friend has been sold on HP products ever since and has purchased some 5,000 dollars worth of HP computers and printers since he received that handwritten note years ago.

Customers Who Won't Shut Up

Lexus is another company with a growing army of customers who won't shut up about how

(Continued)

(Continued)

happy they are. Lexus takes a very systematic approach to finding opportunities to delight. The act of servicing Lexus vehicles follows a different model than those of most other auto manufacturers and dealers. Besides picking up and returning the Lexus owner's vehicle when it requires servicing (and it comes back *washed*), the dealer always calls the next day to verify the level of satisfaction with the servicing. If anything is not right, the dealer returns for the car, takes it back to the garage, and corrects the problem. That in itself is pretty delightful, given the generally abysmal state of auto dealer service. But Lexus is still not finished. It will call *again* and ask "Have we satisfied you this time?"

CREATE A SHARED REALITY

Once the answers to the five big questions about customers are known, you have to make sure that there is a shared understanding about them inside the company.

Do you remember the old story about the three blind men and the elephant? The first blind man felt the elephant's trunk and declared, "An elephant must be a fire hose." The second man felt the elephant's leg and concluded, "An elephant must be a tree trunk." The third blind man touched the animal's tail and said, "You're both wrong; the elephant is like a snake."

In business, different groups of employees, like the three blind men, are inclined to understand the customer in different ways. We can practically guarantee that if representatives from sales, finance, and engineering sit in on the same customer focus group, each will come away with a different understanding of key customer concerns. Their different perceptions are functions of their training and experience. As the saying goes, "If you're a hammer, everything looks like a nail." A diversity of perspectives is a big plus for the enterprise—it creates a multidimensional view of the customer—but those perspectives need to be brought together.

The first step in creating a shared reality is to bring the customer inside the company. Here are just a few notable examples:

- Rohm & Haas, a global chemical firm brings its managers and key customers together for periodic meetings. At these meetings customers explain what they need, what they expect from R&H, what they are not getting, and what its competitors are doing better.
- General Motors, in its electric vehicle project, took a dozen prototypes to several U.S. cities. In each of these locations, the GM project team gave the prototypes to carefully selected individuals to drive for two to four weeks—to the store, to work, wherever regular drivers would go. Over 100 individuals participated in these tests. At the end of the test period, these drivers were debriefed by GM engineers, who learned what they liked, what they disliked, and how the prototype electric vehicle could be improved.
- When Continental Can developed a new technology for molding plastic packaging, it invited one

of its customers—a tennis ball manufacturer—to visit its facility to see if the technology would be useful. At first, the customer failed to see value in the new technology. Before long, however, Continental Can engineers and representatives of the customer found a new way to produce a superior packaging format at a lower cost.

- Steelcase, a leading designer and manufacturer of furniture worldwide, operates like cultural anthropologists. The company observes firsthand how people work in groups, individually, in the office, and in hotels and airports. Steelcase's unique research and development techniques have earned them the reputation as a thought leader on how people work best, as well as the Industrial Design Excellence Gold Award for their Personal Harbor Workspace product.

Simply getting the customer's voice inside the organization, however, is no assurance that the organization will develop a coherent customer understanding. There will still be an inclination for each specialized unit to see a different slice of reality. The best way to avoid this kind of functional myopia is to actually bring the customer and the company's representatives together at the same time to clarify customer requirements. By sitting in the same room, and listening to each other, all of the parties are more likely to come to a shared understanding.

Once a shared customer reality is developed, it must be used to drive the company's work activities, processes, and systems. When this happens we have achieved *total customer focus* (Figure 5-5).

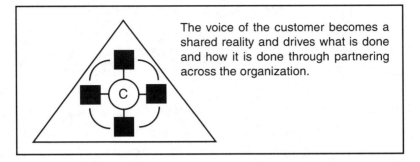

The voice of the customer becomes a shared reality and drives what is done and how it is done through partnering across the organization.

Figure 5-5. Total customer focus.

Once the idea of total customer focus takes root, employee behavior changes for the better. More people take responsibility for gathering customer data and satisfaction.

GET TO YOUR CUSTOMER'S CUSTOMER

The last of the three big factors needed to create horizontal alignment is getting to your customer's customer. Every business, even the simplest, is part of a chain of value creation in which one party's customer is a supplier to some other customer. For example, the customer for an Asian disk drive maker is a California PC maker. The PC maker's customer is a catalog retailer in New Hampshire. The retailer's customer is a school district in Ohio. Horizontal alignment is enhanced to the extent that each link in the chain anticipates the final customer's requirements.

The idea of the customer's customer is particularly relevant within organizations. Everything we've said so far about customers has implied *external* customers. Yet the fact is that most of us are *internal* customers to some fellow employees and suppliers to others. Every employee is part of a chain of internal customers and suppliers that ultimately extends to the external customers. At IBM, the notion of internal customers dates back to the "Basic Beliefs" articulated by founder Thomas Watson. As described by one IBM employee, the objective is "to meet the needs of your customer, and your 'customer' is whomever your work moves to next."

Consider the chain of suppliers and customers described in Figure 5-6. R&D is a supplier to its customer, engineering. Engineering, in turn, supplies its customer, manufacturing. And so on. Even after the product has passed through distribution to the external customer, we're likely to find that this customer is acting as a supplier to another company higher up the chain of value creation. So, most of us play dual roles, as suppliers *and* as customers.

We strengthen horizontal alignment as we learn to think and act on behalf of our customer's customer. If

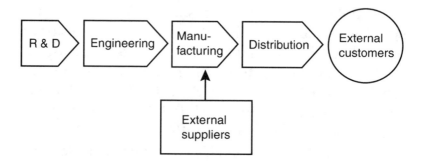

Figure 5-6. Suppliers and customers.

R&D can think beyond the requirements of engineering—its immediate customer—to the packaging problems of the distribution unit and the manufacturing capabilities of the production plant, chances are that its output will sail through the system and enjoy much greater impact in the market.

When you understand your customer's customers, you become a tremendous asset to your more immediate customer, not simply because you are providing a better product or service, but because you are helping the immediate customer do a better job with *its own* customer. Anticipating the requirements of a customer many steps removed, however, is extremely difficult in the unaligned organization.

Three Essentials for Achieving
Horizontal Alignment

1. Determine your customers *care-abouts* and identify new opportunities for satisfying them.

2. Create a *shared reality* within the organization.

3. Understand the needs of your *customer's customer*, those individuals in the customer supply chain that lead up to the final customer.

Reducing Losses

Each supplier-customer interface creates an opportunity for someone to miscommunicate, fail to deliver, or otherwise drop the ball. A few years ago George Labovitz wrote a piece for the *Wall Street Journal* entitled "Keeping Your Internal Customers Satisfied."[4] In it he suggested that suppliers should always ask their internal customers three basic questions:

1. What do you need from me?

2. What do you do with my output?

3. Are there gaps between what you need and what you get?

The day after the article appeared, he received a call from a woman who was in charge of 900 engineers at one of the world's largest computer companies. She explained that none of those engineers dealt with external customers. All of their customers were internal. "When I read your article," she said, "it reminded me of what happens when electrons flow through a wire." Labovitz, a psychologist by training, confessed that he didn't have a clue about how electrons flow through wires, so she explained: "When electrons flow through a wire, they lose energy at each connection." To her, the supplier-customer connection was a clear analogy. "If you can reduce the loss at each connection by asking your three questions, quality and productivity have to go up at the other end!"

Process Improvement

Process improvement concerns the many activities and "connections" that stand between you and "getting to your customer's customer." The process view of work is now fairly well understood by managers in all sectors of the economy. In a nutshell, a process is a series of activities or tasks that are done to add value. Product development is a process because it involves lots of activities that together move product concepts to the marketplace. Fulfillment is another process—it is everything that happens between the time a customer calls with an order and when that customer is satisfied that the transaction has been completed.

Despite our growing understanding of processes, many companies continue to look at activities individually and try to improve them in isolation, without considering their connections to the rest of the business. These companies need to look at the big picture.

Process thinking and improvement is an essential ingredient of horizontal alignment. The goal is to eliminate unnecessary boundaries or connections between different activities and, in so doing, "reduce the loss." We attempt to link as many discrete activities as possible into simple and seamless operations that think and act as one, with the customer—and the customer's customer—in mind. For example, to the extent that we can redesign the activities shown in Figure 5-6 into a *single* process—called "product delivery"—we can bring everyone and everything they do closer to the customer. There are now fewer connections in the wire, so to speak. R&D, engineering, manufacturing, and distribution can all sing from the same score. If we make sure that our processes focus on the customer as the *super*ordinate goal, then we'll have powerful horizontal alignment.

Partnering: Creating a Virtual Organization

The ultimate process improvement—the Valhalla of horizontal alignment—is the situation in which external suppliers and external customers are actually part of the process. When this happens, the last of the decoupling boundaries is eliminated. This is already happening in a number of industries. Most auto makers now bring their parts suppliers into the product development loop at the very beginning. Dell Computers, king of the direct mail PC sellers, brought in its outside shipping vendor, Roadway Express, to manage its entire logistics operation.

A few years ago we facilitated a partnering workshop between Procter & Gamble and Wal-Mart. Sam Walton, the founder of Wal-Mart, and John Pepper, the president of P&G, participated. The purpose of the workshop was to resolve strategic differences that had arisen between the two companies. For example, Wal-Mart wanted just-in-time daily delivery of P&G products to its stores, which would keep a steady stock of these products on Wal-Mart shelves and eliminate costly inventory. This would be a problem for P&G, since Wal-Mart's order pattern did not support full-truck delivery, and sending partial truckloads wouldn't be economic for P&G.

These two giants had a hard time arriving at a deal because each had a different view of the same customer, and each had a different strategy for serving that customer. P&G's strategy was oriented toward periodic sales promotions with special prices, while Wal-Mart pledged everyday low prices.

Eventually, by looking at the final customer—the Wal-Mart shopper—these two companies came to an arrangement that pleased the customer as well as both companies. The companies became partners in a seamless process that served the final customer. The net result of the partnering process was that P&G increased its business with Wal-Mart by 300 percent. By simplifying and streamlining processes that were overlapping or redundant, they, in effect, created a virtual organization to best meet the needs of the final customer.

Since that meeting we've held similar sessions between customers and their suppliers, with the same kind of results. What we have learned from this experience is summarized by our "Five Ps of Partnering":[5]

1. Select the Right Partner.

2. Select the Right Process.

3. Select the Right People.

4. Select the Right Pitch.

5. Select the Right Pfollow-through.

The Right Partner. Since partnering requires an investment of time and effort, be selective. Look for partners who are senior enough to override excuses and drive change; who share your desire or need for breakthroughs; and who have demonstrated a willingness to innovate and achieve win-win solutions.

The Right Process. You can't work on everything at once. So give priority attention to work processes that provide maximum benefit to the ultimate customer; offer the greatest potential return on investment; are perceived as "important" by both parties; could create a competitive advantage for customer and supplier;

and could be improved within a reasonably short time frame.

The Right People. To make the partnering initiative a success, you must bring together the right people to represent both the customer and supplier. By the "right people" we mean key decision makers (of roughly equal rank) from each organization; good listeners; people in a position to implement your idea to improve processes; and creative, positive thinkers.

The Right Pitch. When approaching potential partners, think about their "currencies" (what could a partnering experience provide that they might value?) and position your offer accordingly. Ask yourself: What will make partnering attractive? What data do you need to make this offer compelling? Who should be your first point of contact? What process improvement opportunities do you have in mind? How might successful process improvement benefit the ultimate customer shared by you and your potential partner?

The Right Pfollow-through. The partnering meeting must conclude with an explicit plan. This plan should include the formation of quality action teams comprised of representatives from both organizations; a well-defined methodology for process improvement; clearly defined deliverables; specific measures of success; and a timetable for completion of your objectives.

STAYING ON COURSE

Let's assume that you've done everything right in your business and you've achieved horizontal alignment. You understand who your customers are and what they want. Everyone and every department has played along and lined up their activities in harmony with these understandings. There are no big gaps between what customers expect and what you give them. You are *so* aligned that our firm must award you the coveted Grand Master Alignment Black Belt.

But the game doesn't stop here. Now you have to *stay* aligned, which is tough to do because customers keep changing. Some customers drop out of the market for reasons we can't control—they die off or move away. Industrial customers go out of business and stop buying. Still others change their standards or requirements. Imagine a customer base of pre-adolescents. The half-life of a product concept in that market is probably less than three weeks.

Companies have tried various approaches to sense shifts in customer requirements and satisfaction with current products and services. Sharp, the Japanese electronics firm, placed researchers as boarders in U.S. households to observe how American families use electronic products and to spot opportunities for new ones. Harley-Davidson employs ethnologists to observe the tribal behaviors of motorcycle riders. Most companies use satisfaction surveys like the hotel questionnaires cited above to monitor the mind and mood of customers.

The best monitors of customer alignment are those that give regular feedback. The closer to real-time the better. These make it possible to realign through a series of frequent but small adjustments. If you've ever driven at 70 mph in a car with lots of play in the wheel, you know what we mean. You can't expect to stay aligned if you take a customer satisfaction survey once a year. Frequent, small adjustments will keep you close to alignment all the time and eliminate the need for dangerous course corrections. (For an example of a quick audit that we use to assess the degree to which our clients' organizations are customer focused, see Appendix 4.)

One company we visited recently has a wonderful system for getting regular feedback on internal alignment. It evaluates satisfaction with each internal "supplier" on a weekly basis. Every Friday afternoon, every office employee logs onto a database through his or her desktop computer. A customer survey pops up, asking that employee to rate the services of each department with which he or she has done business during the week on a 1-to-10 scale. How timely was the supplier department? What was the quality of its service? And so on. Every Monday morning, employees return to the database to see how various departments—including their own—have been rated.

Staying Aligned at Fluor Daniel

Fluor Daniel's alignment process—seven years in the making—begins with a shared understanding between Fluor Daniel and their clients and vendors about the *purpose* of a project and assigns seven deliverables that ensure that this purpose is met.

1. *Shared Project Values:* trust, innovation, flexibility, and open communication

2. *A Purpose Statement:* a statement summarizing expected results

3. *Key Result Areas (KRAs):* features objectives such as safety, cost-effectiveness, timely performance, and quality

(Continued)

(Continued)

4. *Measurement:* the mechanism to measure the KRAs already in place

5. *Critical Activities:* the actions necessary to achieve the KRAs

6. *Role Clarification:* clarification of the team's roles and responsibilities

7. *Path Forward:* the identification of action teams and measurement strategies

Keep Your Critics Close

In the Bible, God sent prophets to tell the people of Israel and their leaders of his displeasure. The prophets were loud and clear about what people were doing wrong and how they had better change. Then, as now, no one wanted to hear this criticism, and the prophets were regularly ignored—usually with disastrous results. Likewise, just before the great shipwreck described in the opening of this chapter, a common seaman warned Sir Clowdisley Shovell that by his own reckoning the squadron was dangerously off course. Since navigation by anyone but an officer was considered mutinous, Shovell had the man hanged!

The lesson of the prophets and the mariner is that we often learn the most when we listen to our worst critics. In business, these are often "defectors," people who have tried to do business with us, but who have given up and gone over to the competition. AirTouch Communications, the sixth largest cellular company in the

United States, provides a forum for these defectors at its semiannual customer satisfaction "summits," over which recently retired CEO Lee Cox would preside. "That's another way in which I try [tried] to influence the culture," says Cox. All corporate executives and customer call-center personnel are required to attend. Regular AirTouch subscribers also attend these forums, but defectors are considered special by the company, which flies them in and pays for their hotel rooms. Air-Touch considers the opinion of one defector to be equal to the opinions of 10 regular customers.

Like public sinners, CEO Cox, his management team, and service personnel listened as former customers berated them. "The things they say are stunning," says Cox. "The experience is uncomfortable and awful, but it is just great." In his opinion, the success of a summit is directly related to the degree to which customers and defectors make AirTouch employees squirm.

The AirTouch customer summit would have little value if company personnel simply said *mea culpa* and returned to business as usual. Fortunately, this is not the case. "We were able to identify four or five things that were really key," according to Cox. "[The company is now] going through the second development of our customer satisfaction model. [It has] made huge strides toward continual progress and breakthrough process improvement."

Measurements That Count

Regular and ongoing measurement is our way of sensing our internal environment and the outside world and is the most reliable way of staying aligned. Measurement indicates what is going on with our internal processes and with our customer relationships. It tells us when and where we need to make adjustments.

An old business adage tells us that "if you can't measure, you can't manage." We extend that adage, affirming that what you *choose* to measure has a huge influence on the nature of your business. What managers decide to measure sends a signal to everyone that "this is important." That signal drives the behavior of employees, and that behavior ultimately creates the business culture we end up with. So, if our goal is to create a culture that is naturally self-correcting and self-aligning, we need to be extremely thoughtful about what we decide to measure. (For a comparison of traditional customer focus approaches versus total customer focus, see Appendix 5.)

Our next chapter is dedicated to the subject of measurement. It will show you how just a handful of measures can help you get aligned and stay that way.

6

The Self-Aligning Organization

As a manager, wouldn't it be wonderful if you could flip a switch and put your work team, your department, or your company on autopilot? Freed from the usual steering chores and confident that people would do the right things right, you could spend more time developing the careers of promising employees, interacting with customers, or simply thinking broadly about the future of your business and its markets.

Unfortunately, there is no such thing as organizational autopilot. But using performance measures that are linked to rewards and recognition can do the job, creating what we call the "self-aligning" organization.

A self-aligning organization gets to alignment and stays there, sensing and responding to the barrage of changes that would force the traditional organization off course. It continually monitors itself and the outside environment for indications that the business is on track. Every senior and middle manager, and every employee, gets regular feedback on how things are going and where attention is needed. An "invisible hand" of culture and systems guides everyone in doing the *right* things *right*.

Best of all, the self-aligning organization achieves its purposes without hierarchy and with little micro-management. And its managers—from top to bottom—can sleep at night!

It's possible to push and pull elements of the business into alignment and keep them there through constant craft and attention. But without the characteristics described in this chapter, such organizations will quickly spin out of alignment once key managers release their grip or look the other way.

> The self-aligning company has an "invisible hand" of culture and systems that keeps everyone in the organization doing the *right* things *right*.

Performance measures can be used to monitor and create a self-aligning culture—the nearest thing we know to an organizational autopilot. But before we show you, here are a few questions you should ask with respect to your own organization. Your answers will indicate your company's current state of self-alignment:

1. When customer requirements change, are they picked up by your managers and employees quickly?

2. If a customer makes a serious complaint, is the complaint quickly remedied?

3. When process changes are needed, can the people who manage the operations sense the need and fix them?

4. Are people able to shift gears quickly when market conditions change?

Each of these questions underscores an essential alignment issue: the ability of individuals and departments to sense and respond rapidly to change. If you were unable to say "yes" to each question, this chapter's for you!

INSIDE THE SELF-ALIGNING CULTURE

Federal Express 10:00 A.M. One morning 10 years ago we were working with the senior management group of FedEx on a quality deployment project. At approximately 10:00 A.M., the door of our meeting room swung open and a young man in T-shirt and blue jeans rushed in with a stack of reports under his arm. He handed a copy to CEO Fred Smith and to everyone else in the room. As quickly as he had appeared, the young man was out the door and into the next office, where others were receiving the same report.

Smith and his colleagues quickly shifted their attention from our presentation to the report. Heads nodded around the room as each executive looked over the report. Several smiled and muttered their approval.

Only later did we realize that we had witnessed a daily ritual at FedEx. (Today, the Saturday update is delivered electronically.) Every business day at 10:00 A.M.

local time, every FedEx manager in every one of its offices receives an update of the company's Service Quality Index, or SQI. The SQI is a composite scoring of the tens of thousands of transactions from the previous day, both for the company as a whole and for each local operation. Every damaged package, every late pick-up and incorrect billing, and every failure to make good on the company's guarantee of on-time delivery diminishes the SQI.

Like the senior people in our meeting room, every FedEx manager stops what he or she is doing to read this daily report card when it arrives, since they know that their performance ratings and variable compensation are directly tied to it.

SQI is one of several key measures used by FedEx to stay on top of its operations, its customers, and its position in the fiercely competitive express delivery business. Here are the others:

- *The Customer Service Index (CSI).* CSI tracks customer satisfaction. It asks customers to grade the company on everything from billing procedures to the quality of personnel to on-time delivery.
- *Process Quality Indicators (PQIs).* The company is divided into five core processes: retaining customers; servicing customers; moving, tracking, and delivering packages; invoicing and collecting payment; and providing direction. Each process is monitored with a PQI.

CEO Fred Smith told us recently, "These three dials—the SQI, CSI, and the PQI—are like the altitude, air speed, and attitude indicators. If we manage against them every day, we'll hit our goals." FedEx also puts substantial weight on its "Leadership Index," an employee survey that regularly tracks the quality of how personnel are managed—from the employee's perspective—and the adherence to the company's policy of Guaranteed Fair Treatment. Each unit of the company is wired into these gauges and its own unit measures. Employees don't need to wait for Smith's phone call to identify a problem and take corrective actions. If something is out of line, the company spots it and auto-corrects. FedEx has a culture of measurement, and that culture contributed heavily to its winning the Baldrige Award in 1990, the first service company to do so in the history of the award.

Measurement is a *must* for the self-aligning company.

WHAT TO MEASURE

We are not surprised that Smith, a former Marine pilot, built an organization like an aircraft, with "indicators" and control systems that help him manage the business. He can keep FedEx on course by watching his indicators and fine-tuning the organization through small, periodic adjustments as the company encounters turbulence.

FedEx is not unique. Our experience with dozens of successful organizations—profit, non-profit, and across industries—indicates that measurement is an incredibly powerful tool for *getting* and *staying* aligned. Customer satisfaction measures based on regular surveys, for example, give these companies insights into what they must do to align processes with customer requirements. Once alignment is achieved, the same measures monitor progress and set off warning bells if backsliding occurs. And since people in these companies know what to do and why, they usually get back on track quickly. Indeed, they have clear incentives to do so.

The idea of using measures to monitor performance and stimulate response is not new. Business managers have used quantitative measures for decades—variances from standard costs, output per machine hour, sales per employee, pretax profits, return on equity, to name just a few. As feedback mechanisms, these measures are analogous to the familiar room thermostat, signaling the furnace to send more heat or to stop heating altogether. In the business environment, these signals alert managers when something needs attention. Unfortunately, most traditional measures don't help people feel the true pulse of the business or see where it is heading with respect to things that matter most.

Aligned organizations have a handful of critical indicators that everyone can see and respond to in unison—that directly align intent with action. To UNUM CEO Jim Orr, who likes to sail, these few key measures are like "telltales," the pieces of string that sailors attach high up on the shrouds to indicate apparent wind direction. As Orr says, "They tell you when to tack."

In sailing, the direction of the wind is the most important thing to know, because the wind drives the boat. That's why the helmsman watches the wind like a hawk and responds to its changes. Unfortunately, many of us fail to watch the things that drive the organization—the things that create and sustain success:

customer satisfaction, what employees think about the way they are managed, the effectiveness of core processes. Instead they fixate on lagging indicators like pretax earnings—telltales that explain next to nothing about the customers, employees, and processes that drive their businesses. In the bad old days prior to activity-based costing, managers fixated on machine hours and budget variances, measures that actually sent *false* signals.

> What is needed are measures that align everyone with the intentions of the business and with the key goals of their respective departments.

What wind drives your business? What telltales do you have to sense its strength and direction? Does your department have analogous measures in place? Where should measurement begin?

Always Start with the Main Thing

We showed Fred Smith a list of steps that one company had used successfully to change its culture. Measurement headed the list. Smith looked over the list and nodded his agreement with each step. He then added one caveat. Start, he said, with "the theory of the business"—what we call in this book "the main thing." That is good advice: Measurement is absolutely necessary, but before measurement, managers and employees must have a clear sense of the essence of their business—their main thing.

For Smith, that main thing is absolutely reliable express service, and measures like the Service Quality Index are direct links to it. Jim Orr identifies UNUM's "vision and values" as his main thing and, as we'll see shortly, he has created four key measures to monitor progress toward it.

Stellar Performance

MBNA, one of the country's most successful credit card operations, has the goal of retaining profitable customers. That's its main thing. Given this as the overarching goal, and knowing that premium customers demand premium service, MBNA focuses on a number of process measurements—most relating to speed: how fast employees can process a customer address change; how often the telephone is picked up within two rings; the number of seconds it takes to transfer incoming calls from the central switchboard to the appropriate party. In all, MBNA uses 15 process measures, which are posted daily for all to see. Using these, MBNA manages to retain 98 percent of its customers from year to year.

If we aim to build a self-aligning organization, we must ensure that there is syncronicity between how we measure our business and the essence of the business—the main thing.

Concentrate on the measures that are key to *your* business.

The Importance of Balance

Several years ago, Robert Kaplan and David Norton published an article in the *Harvard Business Review* indicating what managers should measure. Titled "The Balanced Score Card: Measures That Drive Performance," their article affirmed what successful executives have told us: measures should tie back to the company's main thing, in Kaplan and Norton's words, the company's "vision and strategy."[1] With the vision and strategy in mind, they counsel executives to create measures that answer four key questions:

- How do customers see us?
- What must we excel at?
- Can we continue to improve and create value?
- How do we look to shareholders?

Like Fred Smith's main "dials," these measures provide a top-level picture of how the organization is performing. That picture is "balanced" in the sense that, taken together, the four questions help us see the business from the inside *and* the outside, from the perspective of customers, employees, and financial results. Balance is a *must* in any measurement system because organizations are multidimensional. Monitoring performance in a single area to the exclusion of others fails to capture what is going on across-the-board.

Then too, *what we choose to measure has a remarkable effect on behavior,* a fact that many managers overlook. When coupled with reward systems, measurement sends a powerful signal that "the boss thinks this is important." People take very seriously what is measured and tend to ignore other things. So if we measure too narrowly, we create imbalance and potential weakness in the organization. If the boss tells everyone that financial results are all that matter, the boss will probably get what he or she asked for—at least in the short run. But it will also create an environment in which customers and employees don't matter, and in which people will take legal and ethical "shortcuts" in cranking up financial returns.

A friend of ours, an amateur runner, gave us a good example of how measures shape behavior, and how measures too narrowly drawn can undermine performance. He and his running pals were preparing for their first marathon. They relied heavily on the advice of a running magazine that the best preparation for this grueling event was to run *lots of miles* during the weeks prior to the event—*at least* 40 miles per week. With mileage as their measure, our friend's group put in as many miles as possible for three months before the race. Each started recording his mileage in a log, and most felt guilty if they came up short for a given week. "How are your numbers this week?" one would ask another. "Not too good. I've only been averaging six miles per day this week. And I missed two days. I'll have to make up for it with a 15-miler this weekend."

When the big day came, our friend and each member of his group managed to finish the 26.2-mile race. But each was disappointed with his time, which compared poorly with other amateur runners in their respective age groups. The problem, they discovered later, was that mileage is just one of two highly critical measures that more experienced runners use in their training. They had entirely overlooked the other, pacing. More experienced runners gave almost equal weight to training sessions that emphasized speed over short distances. For them, mileage *and* pace training made for superior performance.

In business, we see a similar tendency to concentrate on one or two measures that are not key to the organization, often with the same poor results. For example, a major U.S. automaker used "cost per car" as a key measure. Reducing cost per car became a major priority and was backed by financial incentives. One engineer discovered that if the precious metals in the company's catalytic converters were replaced by some other metal, cost per car would drop by three dollars. The company was so delighted it gave the engineer a bonus and a promotion. Several years later, the company discovered that it was paying a billion dollars a year on warranty costs associated with failures in its catalytic converters. If you guessed that the substitute metal was the cause, you guessed right.

Financial measures are important, but not to the exclusion of others. For any company, department, or team to be successful, it must do well in terms of its customers, operating processes, employees, *and* financial measures. That's why we advocate balance between them.

Dr. Dennis O'Leary understands the power of measurement and its relationship to positive outcomes. As president of the Joint Commission on Accreditation of Healthcare Organizations (JCAHO), he has helped shape the management and measurement practices of the American health care industry. The JCAHO sets standards for health care organizations, and its surveyors evaluate those organizations against those standards. Accreditation is a very serious proposition to the hospitals and other health care organizations undergoing scrutiny. Both reputation and reimbursement are at stake. He states:

> We've aligned our JCAHO standards expectations with the expectations that a good healthy organization would have of itself. And, with the expectations of the people who are provided services and care by that organization. This is not rocket science. What it means is that our standards are focused on the basics; they're focused on the fundamentals of good patient care and good organization management. Because that's all there is.

Characteristics of Key Measures

Measures that are key to *your* business should have these three essential characteristics:

1. They must be broad enough so everyone in the company can understand their individual contribution.

2. They must unify the organization—its culture, systems, processes, and output.

3. They must be future oriented so that they will still be effective as the company grows.

MEASUREMENT IN ACTION

How companies can select a balanced set of measures and use them to create self-alignment is evident in the case of UNUM, an insurance company based in Portland, Maine. Under Jim Orr's direction, UNUM has become one of the fastest growing and most respected companies in the disability insurance industry. Its thoughtful use of measures and goals has played a big part in that success. "When we went public," says Jim Orr, "we had our first key corporate-wide goal, which was defined as '61592.' That was to earn six dollars a share with 15 percent return on equity in 1992." Orr and his employees actually achieved that goal one year ahead of schedule, then got together to develop a new set of goals and measures designed to propel them forward through 1998—the 150th anniversary of the company. The new plan was developed by 13 people from different parts of the corporation. Hundreds of other employees, and a number of outside experts, helped shape it.

In this new plan, UNUM describes its vision and values (its main thing) to be worldwide leadership in its chosen markets and establishes a set of success indicators and goals for pursuing it. Every employee from the executive suite to the lowest level is made aware of the larger vision, the goals, and how his or her contribution to them will be measured.

In developing its measurement system, UNUM adopted an approach similar to the structure tree approach explained in Chapter 4. Such an approach begins with the main thing of the business (or the business unit) and identifies a small set of associated success indicators. Managers then create goals for each indicator. It is then the job of departments, work teams, and individual employees to develop activities and tactics for achieving the goals; these activities and tactics, in turn, have their own measures.

UNUM uses a balanced set of four critical success indicators (our term). The first two, people (employees) and operating effectiveness, provide a look inside the company. The next two, customer satisfaction and shareholder value, provide an external perspective. Each of these four critical indicators, in turn, has an associated goal that identifies and quantifies what the company expects to accomplish (Figure 6-1). Each individual and operating group is charged with finding its own way to achieve these goals.

The entire system of goals, measures, and associated rewards is made clear to employees from top to bottom. Every UNUM employee is given a booklet that explains the overarching goal of the company, its four critical success indicators, and their associated goals (see Appendix 6). And every employee is tied with stock options and other incentives to goal achievement.

MEASUREMENT IS THE KEY TO CULTURE

Years of consulting to many organizations has confirmed for us what psychologists have been saying for years: *Measures shape behavior,* and *behavior creates culture.*

Every organization has a culture, and that culture—for better or worse—is largely determined by what its leaders have chosen to measure and to reinforce with incentives. This is why the choice of measurement is so important; measures eventually determine the behavior of personnel and the culture of the organization.

In rare cases like UNUM and FedEx, we see the kind of self-aligning culture to which every organization

Critical success indicator	**Goal**
Unum PEOPLE We will have the mind of a customer and the pride of an owner.	Our goal is to improve annually on the score established by the benchmark survey. In addition, we will monitor our progress toward this goal on an ongoing basis through formal and informal gathering of employee opinions.
(⊛) A benchmark survey will integrate the company's employee surveys into a tool for gauging progress.	
OPERATING EFFECTIVENESS We will increase customer value by rethinking, improving, and streamlining our business procedures.	By 1998, our total operating costs ratio will be reduced by approximately one-third.
(⊛) Operating costs will grow at no more than one-half the rate of the top line.	
CUSTOMER SATISFACTION Unum will provide the best value in offerings matched to customers' needs in the markets we choose to serve.	We will continually improve our customers' perception of the value of Unum's offerings so that the number of customers who DO NOT rate Unum as "very good" or "excellent" will have declined by 40 percent when we compile our final measurements in 1998.
(⊛) Each Unum area with an external customer chain will develop a customer value measurement tool. It will be aimed at determining our customers' assessment of the overall value of our products and services.	
SHAREHOLDER VALUE We will deliver consistently superior long-term value to Unum shareholders.	We will achieve a total return that consistently places Unum among the top 125 companies listed on the Standard & Poor's 500.
(⊛) Shareholder value will be measured in terms of total return—i.e., dividends plus share price appreciation.	

(⊛) = quantitative measurement

Figure 6-1. Unum's critical success indicators and goals.

should aspire. Here, every employee understands what the organization views as important; and his or her own part in creating success is defined. Daily rituals like the 10:00 A.M. SQI report, as well as rewards and recognition, continually reinforce these understandings. Every part of the system—critical success indicators, stretch goals, and related activities—is hardwired to the main thing of the business. Every manager and every employee gets regular feedback on how things are going and where attention is needed.

And it all starts with measurement.

Stand back and look at your own organization. How many employees can articulate its key objectives? Are measures and rewards tied to these objectives? Can you see the connection between these measures and your own behavior?

Most people don't like measurement and resist it because they associate it with review. But if measures are shown to be meaningful—if someone explains how they relate to the main thing of the business—and if they are linked to rewards and recognition, that resistance can be overcome and people will adapt their behaviors to the measures over time. The collective behavior of people forms a *culture of self-alignment* (Figure 6-2).

The Service Quality Index of FedEx is a powerful example of the measure-to behavior-to-culture process. SQI is meaningful because it is hardwired to the main thing of the business. Everyone at FedEx recognizes that. SQI provides a daily reminder of what is important; it is linked to rewards and recognition for FedEx employees and has clearly shaped the collective behavior and culture of the organization.

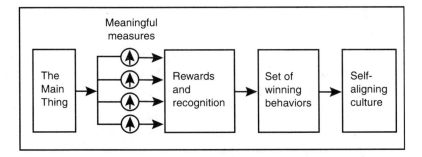

Figure 6-2. Measures shape behavior and behavior creates culture.

Some people who've heard us talk about FedEx and its powerful system of measurement object: "FedEx is a fairly young company, and it grew up with that system. Our company is too set in its behaviors and culture to change." We disagree. Changing behavior is difficult; changing culture requires time. But both can be done, as the following story makes clear.

The Motorola Experience

Today, Motorola Corporation is recognized by people in the quality business as one of the great success stories of the last 20 years. It has a culture of product and process quality that few can match. Six Sigma Quality is the lingua franca of that culture, and every employee, whether he or she is American, German, or Chinese, speaks it fluently.

Motorola wasn't always a quality leader. Far from it, its Asian competitors had bested it all through the 1970s. The story of how it turned that situation around, and in so doing changed its culture, suggests how measures, training, and reward systems can transform even a far-flung enterprise.

Back in 1978, Motorola Corporation found itself in serious trouble. New competitors, primarily in Japan, were invading its markets with high-quality products at reasonable prices. By comparison, Motorola's offerings were often second-rate. Chairman Bob Galvin's response was to issue a Herculean challenge to every unit of his worldwide company: *Improve the quality of your critical processes tenfold within the next five years!*

Galvin's challenge was at first met with inaction. Ten-fold improvement seemed impossible. No one in the company had a clue about how it could be done. We recently asked C. D. Tam, now head of Motorola's Asian operations, what he did when he received Galvin's directive. "Nothing happened for three and a half years," he told us. When we asked why, he laughed and said, "I think we were all hoping that Bob would die or retire!" Galvin did neither. He hung in there and kept hammering on his goal of tenfold process improvement. Forced to take Galvin seriously, Motorola managers took up the improvement challenge and, to their amazement, achieved his tenfold improvement in every critical process in a year and a half.

As described by C. D. Tam, measurement played a key role in reshaping Motorola's culture. In fact, it headed the list of steps used by Motorola to focus attention and change behavior in favor of quality. Those steps were to

- Start with measurement
- Make quality a strategic goal
- Tie measures to performance management
- Train, train, train

- Initiate senior management review
- Create goals for everyone

The behavior of employees and the culture of Motorola today would be practically unrecognizable to a customer or employee from the 1970s. Today, quality is part of the company's DNA. This is clear from everything we've read and from a recent visit to a Motorola semiconductor plant in China. Scattered throughout this plant, electronic scoreboards announce current performance in new customer orders, cycle time, defect rates, and profits. Months in which goals are met or exceeded are celebrated in the plant cafeteria with shark fin soup!

For its Asian operations in general, Motorola now exceeds Six Sigma Quality—less than 3.4 defects per million.

REALIGNING AGAINST CHANGING TARGETS

The concepts we've discussed suggest that once you get aligned on the main thing of your business, and once you've created a culture of self-alignment, you and your co-workers can all settle into a steady state in which only periodic adjustments are required. This is true in part. Over the long haul, major change is usually required—good managers understand this. They know that something big will come along in their markets, in technology, or somewhere else, that will force them to make a major change in direction.

We caught a whiff of this in a discussion with Jim Orr. As he talked to us about his overarching goal of worldwide leadership in disability insurance, we noticed he was deliberately vague about what that meant. This seemed odd, given how everything else in UNUM's measurement/goal system is so clearly defined. "How will you know when you've achieved worldwide leadership?" we asked. His response: He didn't know and wasn't concerned about being specific. Orr was more concerned with creating an organization that could steer efficiently and unerringly to its target—*whatever* that target might be. Today it's disability insurance; tomorrow it might be something else. Opportunities rarely reveal themselves far in advance.

Targets can and must change over time. Old markets fade away and new opportunities appear. In the long term, however, targets are less important than our ability to hit them.

It's certain that Bob Galvin had no idea in the 1970s that Motorola would be making billions of dollars in pagers and cellular communications in the 1990s, just as his father before him could not have known that the car radio company he started in the 1930s would be a major producer of television sets in the 1960s. This company knows that change will shape its future. As Christopher Galvin, Bob's grandson once remarked, "We don't know what it will be, but somewhere out there is going to be a pony to ride."[2] Likewise, FedEx may be a leader in airborne express package delivery today, but who knows what form express delivery will take in the next 10 years?

We submit that the strength of UNUM, Motorola, FedEx, and many other companies has less to do with their current strategies and markets than with their ability to align and deliver even as the main thing of their business changes. In this sense they are like airplanes. They are not programmed to fly to single destinations, but have indicators and guidance systems that make it possible to go wherever the pilot and crew decide to go. With trained crew members and the right systems, they can go anywhere. And so can companies that have mastered the disciplines of alignment.

What You Can Do

Organizations need self-alignment at every level. Department heads, middle managers, and team leaders can create self-alignment in their areas of responsibility, just as the CEO can and should for the organization as a whole. No matter how large or how small your unit, you can take these steps today:

1. *Start with the main thing of the business or your business unit.* Do you know what it is? Do your people know? Don't simply post the main thing. Engage the people who work for you in a dialogue to be sure that they understand it and its implications for their work.

2. *Create your own set of indicators.* No matter where you are in the organization, you have customers (either internal or external), employees, financial requirements, and processes under your direct control. Create a meaningful measure for each. Make each as close to "real-time" as possible.

3. *Make sure that everyone understands your measures and how they tie into the main thing.* Give every person working for you a one-page graphic that shows how his or her work contributes to the main thing. If more than a single page is required, you're not being clear.

4. *Link measures and activities with rewards and recognition.* There should be a pecking order of measures and rewards. Match these to customer "care-abouts." What customers care about most should earn the highest reward.

5. *Give people the training they need to do the job right.* Start by identifying the people who do the job best and the measures that point to "best." What makes them "best"? Train others to be like them.

6. *Create goals for everyone.* Everyone from top to bottom needs individual goals that align with the overarching goals of the department, the division, and the company.

7. *Review performance on a regular basis.* Let customers rate employees through appropriate measures—like the SQI at FedEx. This makes rating more objective and takes the burden off you.

Steps for Creating a Self-Aligning Organization

1. Start with the main thing of the business or your business unit.

2. Create your own set of indicators.

3. Make sure that everyone understands the company's measures and how they tie into the main thing.

4. Link measures and activities with rewards and recognition.

(Continued)

(*Continued*)

5. Give people the training they need to do the job right.

6. Create goals for everyone.

7. Review performance on a regular basis.

We've used a lot of analogies to airplanes and their control systems in this book. Here's one more. The plane needs a pilot. The pilot determines the destination and the best route to it, checks the plane's systems before and during the flight, and intervenes whenever those systems need adjustment. You always need the pilot—pilots *fly* the airplane, they don't make the airplane *fly*.

What we've just described are functions of leadership, the subject of our next chapter.

7

*Distributed
Leadership*

You simply cannot arrive at alignment without leadership, nor can you sustain alignment in its absence. Leadership is the "soft stuff" in the alignment process, but it is the most important. Fred Smith told us, "When it comes to alignment, the hard stuff (measurement) is easy; the soft stuff (leadership) is hard."

The literature on leadership is immense. According to one estimate, over 3,000 books and articles have been published on this topic within the last 30 years alone. This literature contains many practical insights about the traits and behaviors of leaders. Our coverage here focuses on two types of leadership: the type required to get aligned and the type needed to stay aligned.

When the subject of leadership comes up, most people automatically think of a handful of people at the top: the CEO and the senior management team. Strong leadership at the top, as we will demonstrate, is always important, but it is insufficient for sustained success.

Leadership is required at every level, a concept we call "distributed" leadership, which we define as the presence of capable leadership in different units and at different levels of an organization. Distributed leadership is found at the edges of the aligned organization, among men and woman who are both empowered to act and knowledgeable about what must be done. There, it aligns employee activities with the broader goals of the organization. Some companies recognize this form of leadership as a source of competitive advantage. "We can move faster," says Lee Cox, "and we can hit hard issues rather than skirting them. I don't think you can have complete alignment without it."

Distributed leadership is the glue of alignment.

If you can identify a customer, if you have some responsibility for the success of a strategy, if you have employees who look to you for resources and direction, if you control some process—no matter how small—this chapter is for you.

As we began thinking about leadership, we found ourselves turning time and again to the military experience of leadership, which is long and rich in examples. What strikes us most about military organizations are the two very different modes in which they and their leaders operate: peace time and combat. The people, traditions, and hierarchical structures are the same in both modes; what differs remarkably is the way people behave.

If you've ever served in a peace time military unit, you may recall some of its characteristics. First, there is *no compelling mission or threat* to galvanize effort or stir emotions. Lacking these, the objective is preparedness and self-maintenance. Thus, peace time units engage in periodic training and busywork: cleaning equipment, spit-shining boots, preparing reports, and other activities, few of which have anything do with the business that military units are established to do.

Second, things are done "by the book" or "by the numbers." There is a tremendous emphasis on SOPs (standard operating procedures), with little left to the imagination or discretion of the individual soldier. Hierarchy and the pecking order of authority are central to the system and are reinforced in a number of ways: for example, communications have to pass up and down the chain-of-command.

Those of us who've served in peace time military units can recall the attitudes that prevailed in these conditions, especially in the lower ranks: boredom, lots of grousing, occasional malingering, and "looking out for Numero Uno." This is not a pretty picture, but most former servicemen and women would describe peace time military life as we have here.

Put these same units and individuals into a combat situation, however, and just about everything changes! Military formality becomes the first casualty. Hierarchy continues to exist on paper, but it is quickly replaced by *organic* behavior. The mission is painfully clear: Find the enemy, fight the enemy, and win. People quickly forget their differences and bond together around this overarching goal. They find themselves doing things they never thought they had the courage or strength to do. People who were bored become fully engaged and emotionally charged.

And leadership breaks out all over. Small unit commanders—captains, lieutenants, and sergeants—find themselves in situations in which they must do their own thinking and their own acting. Guided by their training and their understanding of the mission, however, they know what to do and how to do it. They are prepared to think and to act. If they become casualties, others step in to take their places, guided by the same understanding.

It is not surprising to us that the aligned companies we have described in this book—FedEx, Motorola, UNUM, Southwest Airlines, JPL, AirTouch, and others—all operate in combatlike environments where competition is intense, change is rapid, and no one knows what the future will look like. These companies have hierarchies, but don't act as though they're governed by them. They respond to their hostile environments like combat units—rapidly and in organic ways. And their employees seem genuinely excited about what they're doing.

In contrast, misaligned companies act like peace time armies. They lack clear objectives around which everyone can rally; they make everyone operate by the book; employees don't see the purpose of their work or the value they add to it, so they are either bored or uninvolved. Strong leadership exists only at the top; elsewhere, routine is its surrogate.

Which does your company act like: the peace time or combat unit? Which would you prefer to emulate? We often ask managers who have had military experience this question. "Would you rather work in an organization that functioned like a peace time military unit or a combat unit?" The answer is always unanimous—combat! Why? Here are the usual answers:

1. "We had a clearly defined objective." Often, they relate, the lower levels of the organization had clearer goals than the top.

2. "There was a heavy commitment to the team and to each other." Combat units are like clocks. All the pieces have to work. Functional interdependence creates psychological interdependence as well. It represents a time and an experience for some where there really was something worse than death—not "keeping the faith," and letting the team down.

3. One manager told us, "There was more leadership and less 'chicken-ship' in combat units." In other words, there was less status differentiation, less hierarchy, because everyone was in the same boat.

4. "There was lots of two-way communication." In contrast to the stereotype about the one-way directedness of military communication ("Jump and I'll tell you how high!"), in combat there is an ebb and flow of information.

Remember, combat units are social systems trying to survive in a hostile environment. These people and their units had to be aligned in order to survive. Their missions were clear. People understood the strategy and their part in it. Everything was on the line for them, and they could fall back on their training to do the job.

How can we get our business organizations to act with this commitment and this level of organic effort? The answer is *leadership*. The leader—whether it is the CEO or the front-line supervisor—can do it if he or she will do the following:

- *Keep people continually connected to the hostile environment in which they operate.* They must understand what is at stake.
- *Help people to think holistically.* In the distributed environment we hope to build, we cannot expect employees to make good decisions and do the right things if they cannot see the big picture.
- *Always keep people connected to the main thing of the entire business,* not of some limited departmental goal.
- *Reward and recognize people for working toward the main thing.* If you reward people for pursuing departmental goals only, you'll find people creating deeper silos.
- *Use the review process to carry the message to employees.* The measures against which you review people will drive future behavior.
- *Create opportunities for people to interact.* People work together effectively when they personally know and empathize with other individuals.

Fred Smith summarized the issue of leadership and the military when he told us the following:

Most of the time the military gets the bad rap. . . . I know a lot about the military, and the military that works best is very collegial, very much mission focused, very much built around good leadership principles. I can absolutely assure you that the U.S. Marine Corps, of which I'm an alumnus, has forgotten more about leadership than most corporate elements ever will know. And the fundamental part of the leadership is not somebody getting salutes, it's about taking care of the people that do the job—the troops.

> Leadership at the top and at the edges of the organization is essential to getting and staying aligned.

A PUSH FROM THE TOP

Getting to alignment doesn't just happen. Someone in a position of power has to make it happen with a big push or some type of Herculean effort. Real change almost always starts at the top. Change leaders may echo the sentiments and aspirations of lower-level employees—and they must draw their inspiration from what is happening on the front lines—but the ball starts rolling from the top.

If you are not convinced of this fact, consider the corporate makeover of Xerox under David Kearns, Ford under Donald Petersen, General Electric under Jack Welch, and Motorola under Bob Galvin. Each identified something big that needed doing, articulated it clearly, and turned up the heat to be sure that things got cooking. Each succeeded, in most cases with the same cast of employees, which goes to show that people aren't the problem. Under Petersen, for example, the same designers, the same engineers, and the same plant workers who turned out clunky, unremarkable, and poorly built Ford cars all through the 1970s produced the highly acclaimed Taurus in the 1980s—the car that saved Ford from a close encounter with the grim reaper. What produced the improved result? Answer: leadership that identified the threat, rallied people around a focused counterattack, and gave everyone an opportunity to contribute.

To Get People to Contribute, Drive Out Fear

Years ago, W. Edwards Deming made Drive Out Fear one of his 14 principles of quality management. The value of this principle has not dimmed with the years. If you want people to be committed and to contribute, make it safe to do so. The results are often remarkable. The Ford Motor Company case provides a good example.

In his book, *A Better Idea*, Donald Petersen explains how fear constrained employees at Ford's design center from creating the breakthrough designs that training and experience had taught them to make. During a visit to the design center, he recalls, "I was disappointed with what I saw. . . . I asked them if they liked the new cars they were working on [these included the 1983 Thunderbird]. . . . They said that they didn't, and we talked about why. It had a lot to do with lists of restrictions—assumptions about what they could or could not do, based on past experience and a general sense of resignation. That's when I asked them if they would design a 1983 Thunderbird that they would be proud to drive and to park in their driveway."*

Freed by Petersen from the fear of displeasing powerful barons and review committees within Ford, the design staff created a groundbreaking new Thunderbird. The same group departed again from conventional wisdom in its design of the award-winning Taurus, which many in the company's marketing department feared was too radical for its traditional buyers.

(Continued)

(Continued)

Far from offending the buying public, the Taurus's aerodynamic design put Ford out ahead of all foreign and domestic rivals and helped it become the biggest-selling car in America.

———————

*Donald E. Petersen and John Hillkirk, *A Better Idea: Redefining the Way Americans Work* (Boston, Mass.: Houghton Mifflin Co., 1991), 18.

Leadership in Unfriendly Territory

Ideally, the energy and inspiration for alignment originates at the level of the CEO and works down. This doesn't always happen. Let's face it, sometimes senior management just doesn't get it, or doesn't get it soon enough. The failure of corporate-level leadership to provide alignment is not, however, an impediment to lower-level managers and supervisors who want to take responsibility for aligning their own units. Unit-level alignment can be accomplished in spite of what goes on around it, even in "unfriendly territory." And we must confess that we found one of the best lessons for this inside our own company, Organizational Dynamics, Inc. (ODI).

Like other consulting companies, we have a publications department that is responsible for developing and printing materials for training seminars, client presentations, and for sales and marketing purposes. This 25-person department was led by a very competent director, Genoa Shepley. Genoa and her colleagues were always under siege by internal customers, each of whom had special needs and expected priority treatment. Clearly, managing this department was a difficult job. Senior management (us) had declared a zero-defects standard, and the department was saddled with competing demands for resources.

So, what did she do?

For starters, she familiarized her subordinates with the strategy of the company and how their materials helped our company succeed. Internal customers were interviewed so that their needs would be understood clearly by all concerned. These customers explained how they used the publications, giving publications personnel insights into "the customer's customer."

She then created new processes for getting the work done right. These took the form of several "skunkworks," each organized around a company project that required publication services. By design, these skunkworks were highly flexible, and individuals moved frequently from one skunkwork to another. Every Monday morning, in fact, members of the department met to evaluate existing customer demands, and skunkwork teams were regrouped to meet these needs. Since different jobs required different skills—text development, graphics, Macintosh versus DOS platforms, and so forth—people were moved frequently. Wednesday became "review day"; the current situation was assessed, and personnel were regrouped again as necessary.

Everything in Genoa's department was fluid and constantly recalibrated. Whenever she had doubts about her department's own processes and priorities, Genoa told her customers, "This is what we are doing. Does it match up with your needs?"

In terms of our own definition of alignment, this manager and her employees were doing everything right:

- The main thing of the company was clear, and every member of the department saw how his or her work contributed.
- The department was vertically aligned. It had a strategy that everyone understood. And that strategy matched up with what ODI as a company was trying to accomplish. Personnel were regularly sent to seminars and workshops to keep their skills at the leading edge of electronic publishing.
- The department was horizontally aligned. Everyone understood the requirements of internal customers and of their "customer's customers." Flexible and efficient processes were in place to serve them. Genoa constantly benchmarked her department's processes and technologies against those of other outstanding organizations.

The newly aligned publications department mastered its workload with amazing agility, getting printed, digital, and graphic material out on time and with zero defects—something that benchmarking studies indicated our competitors could not do. The skunkworks operation developed by Genoa Shepley taught us a valuable lesson about how leadership can get the ball rolling on its own anywhere in the organization. Whether it comes from the top, the middle, or somewhere else, positive leadership and energy are required to move people to action.

STAYING IN TUNE

While the initial push must come from the top, alignment is only sustained when leadership at other levels is engaged. A forceful leader at the top can briefly muscle together all the key elements that create alignment—strategy, people, customers, and processes—but without leadership at lower levels and across operating units, they will soon lapse into misalignment.

Have you ever watched a flock of geese winging southward on its winter migration? The familiar V-shaped formation makes it possible for all but the lead goose to "draft" behind the bird just ahead, saving a great deal of energy. The lead goose sets the pace and the direction for the entire flock, but eventually it tires. When it becomes too tired to carry the lead, it peels off and forms up in the draft of the last bird on one arm of the V. Another goose at the front takes its place as the lead bird. Each bird knows the direction; each is capable of taking its turn at the vanguard. And each member of the flock has confidence in the ability of its fellow geese. The flock operates as an organic unit.

James Belasco and Ralph Stayer have described the geese flock as a paradigm for leadership:

> What I really wanted in the organization was a group of responsible, interdependent workers, similar to a flock of geese. . . . I could see the geese flying in the "V" formation, the leadership changing frequently, with different geese taking the lead. I saw every goose being responsible for getting itself to wherever the gaggle was going, changing roles whenever necessary, alternating as a leader, a follower, or a scout. . . . I could see each goose become a leader.[1]

The behavior of flocking geese is a metaphor for our notion of distributed leadership. Business organizations need distributed leadership to stay aligned. As Daryl Ferguson once told us, "We need leadership on the front line. I don't want them to be simply empowered, I want them to be aggressive, understanding the goals of the organization above them. Their voice in alignment has to be as strong as top management's."

Earlier chapters describe the importance of having a system of goals and measures throughout the organization as instruments of self-alignment. But someone must be there to articulate the goals and to interpret the performance measures. That is where distributed leadership comes in. Who should these distributed leaders be? If you can identify a key customer, if you have some responsibility for the success of a strategy, if employees look to you for resources or guidance, if you control a process—no matter how small—you should be a leader. You can make a difference.

Distributed leadership makes it possible for people like Genoa Shepley to contribute to the overall business by aligning their own operations—no matter how small or how large. It also safeguards the future of the organization. In military organizations, widely distributed leadership is a must, if only to avoid the possibility of having leadership and control wiped out in a single stroke. This is something that the Iraqi armed forces failed to understand prior to the Gulf War, and they paid dearly for it. Iraqi leadership was bound up in the person of Saddam Hussein and a small coterie of senior officers. Command and control of its air defenses and ground forces were held tightly in their hands, with the reins passing through various fixed communications centers. Knowing this, the Allied forces followed a "decapitation" strategy aimed at severing the head from the body of the Iraqi forces. By all accounts, pinpoint bombing of Iraqi radar controls and communications centers did exactly this. After the initial weeks of the air war, Iraqi's air defense controls had been mostly knocked out, leaving the skies open to day and night attacks. At the same time, communication links between the Iraqi high command and its forces were so badly disrupted that its armored and infantry units sat passively in desert positions, where they were defeated in detail.

In contrast to the Iraqi case, Israeli commanders during the Six Day War of 1967 were given tremendous discretion. Particularly in the Sinai peninsula, where warfare was highly mobile and fast-changing, local tank commanders had to quickly size up the situation and make decisions. There wasn't time to explain the situation to the generals far in the rear and then wait for orders. Fortunately for the Israelis, these commanders were well-trained and understood the larger objectives. The generals knew them and trusted them to work within the broad outlines of strategic plans.

Distributed leadership—in war and business—reduces the risk of concentrated leadership and speeds decision making. At the same time, it creates an environment in which the people at the top can sleep at night, knowing that competent hands are at the wheel and able to do the right thing on their own.

How to Create Distributed Leadership

Developing people who can assume leadership for their business units, their departments, and work groups is one of the most important things a manager can do. This goes beyond simply telling people that they are "empowered."

Stellar Performance

In 1994, Les McCraw at Fluor Daniel set about creating a major cultural change in his company. With the company's recent successes, Les was concerned that they were in danger of becoming arrogant, bureaucratic, and unresponsive to their clients. He felt the way to change culture and empower people was to create objectives designed to support such goals. To cement the new culture, he did the following:

- Mandated greater individual responsibility, expanding the spending authority of unit managers. According to Les, "People who had $1 million authority on Friday discovered they had $10 million on Monday. They also had the sobering realization that their accountability increased ten-fold."
- Told executives that they could live anywhere they wanted as long as they were close to their customers. By doing so he changed the feeling and the role of corporate headquarters.
- Dispersed corporate services in order to better serve the changing company. For instance, the legal department became "Legal Services" and took their new name and identity to heart as they served internal customers.

(Continued)

(*Continued*)

> • Celebrated the actions that reinforced the new culture. According to Les, "It's critical to find good examples, to honor them and celebrate them because you can come up with all the theory in the world, but it doesn't resonate unless you can look to specific examples."

"Empowerment is an unfortunate word," wrote Gordon Sullivan, former army chief of staff, "because leadership is not about power or authority."

[It] is about responsibility—both responsibility delegated and responsibility accepted. Empowered subordinates accept responsibility for themselves, for their team, and for their contributions to the organization. From that sense of shared responsibility come self-confidence, motivation, and commitment. Leader development—investing in people—is about creating that kind of empowerment.[2]

The military approach advocated by Sullivan for developing distributed leadership is based upon values and three main ingredients: education and training, on-the-job experience, and self-development. Using this approach, every military leader is charged with developing the leadership skills of his or her subordinates through counseling, coaching, and feedback. Great business leaders do the same. At Boston-based Gillette, for example, CEO Al Zeien estimates that he reviews the career plans of over 800 managers each year.[3] UNUM's Jim Orr does the same, personally overseeing the career development of 200 or so senior managers. Managers at every level need to do the same for their reports.

The task of creating distributed leadership becomes easier if managers do two relatively simple things:

Hire the right kind of people

If you want people who can be trusted to do the right thing, hire people who are temperamentally disposed to do what you want. For example, Southwest Airlines wants employees to bend over backwards for its customers. This is part of SWA's main thing. To make sure that this happens, SWA hires people who are disposed to be helpful. "We look for people who are unselfish and altruistic," says CEO Herb Kelleher. "We can train anybody to do a job from a technical standpoint. We're looking for an esprit de corps, and attitude. We try to hire and promote people who have a human approach."[4] FedEx also puts tremendous emphasis on leadership, expecting employees with management aspirations to exhibit leadership capabilities from the "get go."

What can happen when you hire the *wrong* people is amusingly told by Dwight Gertz, recounting the case of a shopping mall cookie franchise that could not understand why some stores were highly profitable while others were just the opposite. It was a formulaic, by-the-numbers kind of business. Its operating manual was field tested down to the smallest detail: what kind of cookies to bake, when to bake them, and in what quantities. If the store manager simply followed the manual and his or her training, a profit would result. So why were some stores unprofitable? His investigation found that the problem was not in the cookie stores but "in the corporate human resources department of the conglomerate that owned the cookie store chain. When HR functionaries advertised and interviewed store manager candidates, they touted the job's independence: 'Be an entrepreneur. Run your own business.' " Not surprisingly, they hired people who were not disposed to follow the company's proven formula for profits.[5]

Make "empowerment" more than a slogan

Ever since empowerment became a fashionable term in business, corporations have been telling employees that they are empowered. But few companies, and few employees, have been satisfied with the result. Managers complain, "We give them some discretion, and look what they do. We can't trust them to make the right decisions." Employees complain that managers constantly second-guess their decisions or call them on the carpet for doing something the managers disagree with.

To make empowerment work, recognize that it's a two-way street. First, bosses need to spell out the boundaries within which employees can make their own decisions. Second, employees need to assure bosses that they are capable of making the right decisions. The first is easy. Ritz-Carlton Hotels gives every employee a dollar amount he or she can spend in satisfying a hotel guest. SWA's Kelleher sets no dollar amount, but makes the boundaries of empowerment clear nevertheless: "We tell [employees] to go out and do what they think is right for the customers. In some cases, they may go a little overboard, but they don't get executed for their effort. If their intention is to help a customer, we tell them to just do it, don't worry about it."[6]

For bosses to be assured that employees will make the right decisions, we recommend that boss and employee agree on a *process* for making decisions, which includes

- Criteria for decision making—the decision should serve a key goal of the company or the business unit
- The assumptions and information upon which decisions will be made
- Who should be consulted as decisions are made

This process, together with the establishment of clear boundaries, will head off most of the problems associated with empowerment. Bosses will be less nervous about what their people are doing, and employees will gain greater confidence in their ability to act.

Leadership Behaviors Essential to Alignment

Create Shared Purpose

- Help others understand

  What must be accomplished

  Why their work is worthwhile

  How they can accomplish their goals

Get Commitment

- Increase people's sense of personal ownership for the work they do.
- Drive out fear to improve performance.

(Continued)

(*Continued*)
- Help yourself and others visualize high performance.

Integrate the Organization

- Make information readily available to everyone and avoid the tendency to control information.
- Design networks of relationships to promote flexibility and high performance.
- Help groups integrate conflicting views to achieve technically superior and fully supported outcomes.

LEADERSHIP AS A SOURCE OF ENERGY AND URGENCY

Like machines and living organisms, businesses require energy to stay alive and functioning. And it seems to us that the higher the level of energy in a business, the greater the level of activity and results. We often remark to each other and to our colleagues how the energy level of the companies we visit in our consulting practice is a useful indicator of how well that company is doing. Those that operate on a high charge of energy practically sparkle with enthusiasm and confidence; people are excited about what they're doing. Companies with low energy levels act the opposite.

Energizing the system is a key task of leadership—from top to bottom. When this doesn't happen—or when it stops—the activity of the organization simply winds down like a spring-driven clock. Athletic coaches have understood this for as long as there have been halftimes and locker rooms. Anyone who has been an athlete understands just how much energy great coaches can put back into a team that is down in the dumps. They can pump the team up like pumping up a balloon.

But neither athletes nor balloons will stay pumped up without active management involvement. We observed this during a recent visit to a Japanese tool and die company. Until several years ago, when the U.S. tool and die industry rebounded with remarkable vigor, this company had been doing extremely well. But in the fast-paced 1990s, it was having trouble motivating people around changing technologies and customer requirements. People were confused by all the change and responded by sitting on their haunches. "Our greatest strength in the past had been our ability to gain consensus around a goal," one executive told us.

> But with change now happening so rapidly, our strength has become a weakness. We can't get people to move from one strategy to another, and move quickly. When I visit one of our plants, I can get people there excited. But once I leave that plant, they revert to their old strategy. I am constantly pushing them toward the new strategy and using lots of energy to do so. But it all dissipates once I leave.

This executive eventually found a solution, by holding weekly meetings in which every employee interacted with others on a single subject: the company's strategy. This took tremendous time and effort, but it rekindled energy and enthusiasm around the new strategy. If, as a leader, you want to energize the organization, you have to spark it with your *own* energy.

One of our clients has taken a surgical supply business from $27 million to $127 million in four years. When we asked him to explain his philosophy, he said, "I flood the organization with information and inject a sense of urgency." The message of urgency was repeated in every interview we conducted. For these outstanding executives, the issue at hand was not minimizing risk, but taking action.

Lee Cox said. "*Not* doing something bold in new distribution channels is extremely high risk around here. Doing something isn't risky at all. . . . It's like going to a county fair and throwing balls to win a doll. The more you throw, the more likely you're eventually going to win. If you just stand there and watch, I can tell you for sure, you'll never ever win one of those dolls."

UNUM's Jim Orr said much the same thing: "Who knows what the future looks like in this crazy atmosphere? We haven't the foggiest notion. The key thing is if you can keep practicing all the time by changing, doing things differently, and having intellectual excitement in an institution, you're much better positioned for the big hiccup, which will always come. It always does, because that's life." When we asked him his view on injecting a sense of urgency he exclaimed, "I tell my folks to get on with it. Just do it! You know you're going to be wrong sometimes but that's O.K. too. Just do it. *Not doing it is the risk.*"

Leaders kindle energy in the system by getting people to communicate. That energy typically comes through social interaction. Good leaders understand that people are social animals and create opportunities for them to interact, share information, and generate their own enthusiasm. John Kotter's study of 15 of the world's best managers indicated that these individuals spent 90 to 95 percent of their time out of their offices, interacting with people at every level and in every function.[7] *They worked the crowd.* They move information between turfdoms, connecting different units and creating energy and alignment in the process. Alignment between the parts of the organization requires pushing against a natural tendency for the parts to stand alone. And leaders are the ones to do it.

Dennis O'Leary had this to say:

> I think something as basic as communication requires *affirmative energy* and action.
>
> . . . A lot of people don't even know it's important to communicate. Among those who do know it's important to communicate, there are lots who don't know how to do it. You have to be able to mobilize people behind where you want to get them. You've got to set a target for them, tell them that's the target we're headed for, folks, and get them on board to believe in it. You have to build a culture that supports continuous improvement toward that goal. If you don't do that, you're probably not going to be around here tomorrow.

We like Dennis's use of the term "affirmative energy," because it captures the kind of proactive leadership that is required to get aligned and to stay aligned.

Sam Walton understood this intuitively. He had a fundamental rule for Wal-Mart managers: Corporate managers should be out in the stores, and store managers should be out on the floor. One store manager learned the point of this rule the hard way. In an unannounced visit to this manager's store, Sam found the aisles cluttered and dirty. Going directly to the lumber department, he picked out a sheet of plywood, a hammer, and some nails, and commenced to seal off the door to the store manager's office. Sam gave him the hammer and some advice—spend less time in your office, and stay out *entirely* until you've gotten this store into tip-top condition.

Arriving at alignment is not easy, and every organization must find its own way. But the outcome is worth the effort. (The complete picture of the self-aligning organization is shown in Appendix 7.) Once a company is aligned, managers will spend less time stressing over what their employees are up to and more time on the future of the business. Employees will know what to do and have the green light to do it. Customers will be surprised and delighted with what they're getting. Financial results will follow.

BACK TO THE COCKPIT

We end this book as we began it, in the airplane cockpit—our analogy for the aligned organization. The pilot—the leader—is there among the instruments and crew members and, having done a pre-flight checkout, is confident of the equipment. Because the pilot has shared the flight plan with them, the crew knows what to do and will work together on the journey.

The pilot knows to regularly check the key indicators and keep track of the weather ahead, so that the plane and all aboard will reach their destination safely. If conditions require a change in course or destination, the pilot has the confidence of knowing that plane, pilot, and crew can do it.

That's alignment.

POSTSCRIPT

We certainly hope you enjoyed reading and thinking about the new concept of alignment. We are continuing our research by tracking data from organizations around the world. We would welcome your thoughts, experiences, and ideas.

In addition, if you would like information on ODI's Alignment Diagnostic Profile, please call us at 617/272-8040 or visit our web site at http://www. orgdynamics.com.

Appendices

1

Alignment Diagnostic Profile— Short Version

SELF-DIAGNOSIS

Chapter 3 includes the short version of our alignment diagnostic profile and the alignment snapshot for mapping its evaluation. Here we repeat blank versions of both figures so that you can diagnose the alignment of your own organization.

Perceptions of current organizational alignment vary from person to person. Everyone sees the organization through a slightly different lens. So you might want to have other colleagues—preferably in different departments or business units—participate independently in the diagnosis. If you do, average their scores for each alignment dimension. Doing so will give you a composite diagnosis.

Instructions

Respond to each statement by circling the number (from 0 to 10) that best represents your opinion. If a statement does not apply to you, or you have no opinion, write in N/A (not applicable).

Once you have completed and scored the questionnaire, total the scores for each of the four sections. Then map your scores on the alignment diagnosis snapshot that follows (Figure A-1). For example, if you scored "20" on the strategy dimension, put a dot midway between 40 and 0 on the strategy segment (remember that higher scores are closer to the center). Then connect the dots to create a visual diagnosis of your organization's alignment.

How well-aligned is it? Is it strong in some dimensions and weak in others?

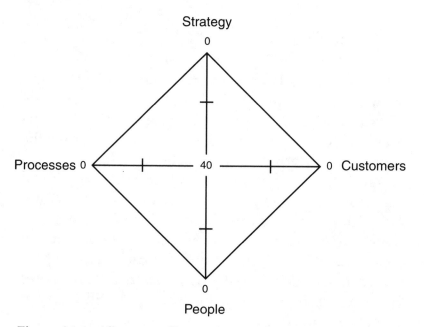

Figure A1-1. Alignment diagnostic snapshot.

Table A1-1. Alignment Diagnostic Profile (short version).

Strategy	Strongly disagree										Strongly agree
Organizational strategies are clearly communicated to me.	0 1 2 3 4 5 6 7 8 9 10
Organizational strategies guide the identification of skills and knowledge I need to have.	0 1 2 3 4 5 6 7 8 9 10
People here are willing to change when new organizational strategies require it.	0 1 2 3 4 5 6 7 8 9 10
Our senior managers agree on the organizational strategy.	0 1 2 3 4 5 6 7 8 9 10

Total ☐

Customers

For each service our organization provides, there is an agreed-upon, prioritized list of what customers care about.	0 1 2 3 4 5 6 7 8 9 10
People in this organization are provided with useful information about customer complaints.	0 1 2 3 4 5 6 7 8 9 10
Strategies are periodically reviewed to ensure the satisfaction of critical customer needs.	0 1 2 3 4 5 6 7 8 9 10
Processes are reviewed regularly to ensure that they contribute to the attainment of customer satisfaction.	0 1 2 3 4 5 6 7 8 9 10

Total ☐

People

Our organization collects information from employees about how well things work.	0 1 2 3 4 5 6 7 8 9 10
My work unit or team is rewarded for our performance as a team.	0 1 2 3 4 5 6 7 8 9 10

(Continued)

Table A1-1. Alignment Diagnostic Profile (short version) (*Continued*)

People (*cont'd.*)	Strongly disagree										Strongly agree
Groups within the organization cooperate to achieve customer satisfaction.	0	1	2	3	4	5	6	7	8	9	10
When processes are changed, the impact on employee satisfaction is measured.	0	1	2	3	4	5	6	7	8	9	10

Total ☐

Processes

	Strongly disagree										Strongly agree
Our managers care about *how* work gets done as well as about the results.	0	1	2	3	4	5	6	7	8	9	10
We review our work processes regularly to see how well they are functioning.	0	1	2	3	4	5	6	7	8	9	10
When something goes wrong, we correct the underlying reasons so that the problem will not happen again.	0	1	2	3	4	5	6	7	8	9	10
Processes are reviewed to ensure they contribute to the achievement of strategic goals.	0	1	2	3	4	5	6	7	8	9	10

Total ☐

©1996 Organizational Dynamics, Inc.

2

Examples of Structure Trees— Citizens Utilities

The following figures are examples of how the structure tree can be used to capture on one page the essence of a business. Citizens Utilities is a major provider of electricity and telecommunications products and services.

Figure	Topic
A2-1	Citizens Utilities 1994 Executive Structure Tree.
A2-2	Citizens' 1995–1997 goals, targets, and measures building off the 1994 Executive Tree.
A2-3	Business Plan Alignment for Western Region Telephone Operations as they built upon corporate goals. For example, see Goal 1A1 (Figure A2-2), "Through target excellence, Citizens will be the employer and supplier of choice." At the Western Region level, it breaks into components, one of which is "Design and implement training plan for WRTO" (Figure A2-3). That results in

targets and a set of measures that can be seen on the
structure tree.

A2-4　1995 Business Plan Goals for Kauai Electric, broken
down by Corporate, Sector, and Division. Each level
took Goal 1A1, "Through target excellence, Citizens will
be the employer and supplier of choice," from the Executive Structure Tree (Figure A2-1) and broke it down
into meaningful subgoals with measures.

A2-5　Additional examples of how a structure tree can cascade
and　strategy down through an organization to ensure align-
A2-6　ment.

1994 Executive Structure Tree

Goals	Year End 1995–1997 Targets	Measures
Customer		
GOAL 1: Through Target Excellence, Citizens will be the employer and supplier of choice.		
1A: Supplier of Choice	100% of Citizens is within 10% of the best by year-end 1996.	• Customer Satisfaction Index Scores
1B: Employer of Choice	Employee Satisfaction Index 8.0 by year-end 1996. Cut in half the difference between 1994 current survey results and 8.0 by year-end 1995.	• Employee Satisfaction Index
Process		
GOAL 2: Identify key processes by year end 1994. By year-end 1996 manage, analyze, and improve processes.	• Rewards and Recognition • Service Initiation Process • Marketing	• Employee Satisfaction Index • Cross-selling Success • Activation Speed • Percent Revenue from New Business Segments
Alignment		
GOAL 3: By year-end 1996, include all employees in developing, implementing, and tracking goals and measures that are aligned with the corporate goals.	• For the 1996 Business Plan involve all exempt employees. • For the 1997 Business Plan involve all employees.	• % of employees involved a) developing b) implementing c) measuring
	• By year-end 1995 employees involved in goal setting will achieve a satisfaction index of 7.0. • By year-end 1996 employees involved in goal setting will achieve a satisfaction index of 7.5.	• % of employees satisfied with involvement in goal-setting process
Financial		
GOAL 4: Continuation of annual increases in corporate revenue, earnings and earnings per share.	• 1995 % ROI Corporate • 1995 OIBIT $ M - $ M • ROI by Sector to be in the top quartile of Sector Benchmark Companies	• ROI • OIBIT

Figure A2-1. Citizens Utilities.

1995–1997 Mission Statement: World class employees dedicated to customer satisfaction

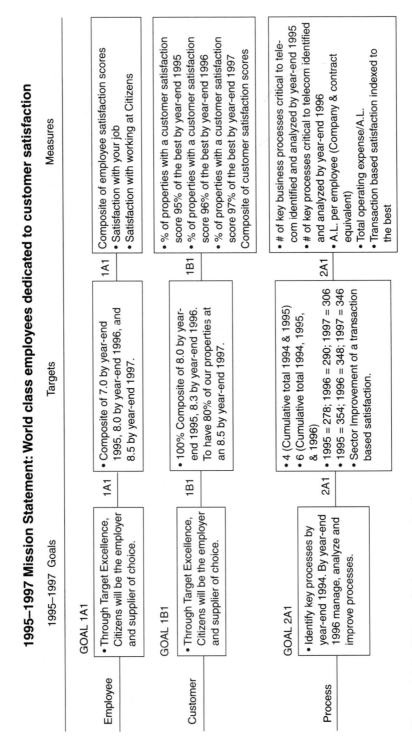

Figure A2-2. Citizens Telecommunications.

BUSINESS PLAN ALIGNMENT—TELECOMMUNICATIONS
Western Region Telephone Operations

Mission Statement: WRTO QUALITY LEADERSHIP TEAM GOALS 1995–1997
World-class employees dedicated
to customer satisfaction.

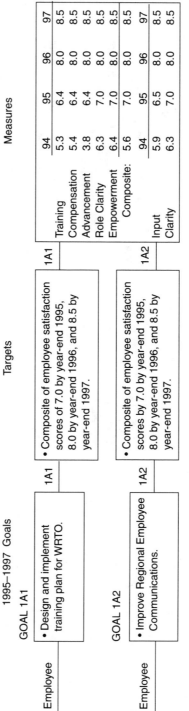

1995–1997 Goals   Targets   Measures

GOAL 1A1

Employee | 1A1 — • Design and implement training plan for WRTO.

1A1 • Composite of employee satisfaction scores of 7.0 by year-end 1995, 8.0 by year-end 1996, and 8.5 by year-end 1997.

	94	95	96	97
Training	5.3	6.4	8.0	8.5
Compensation	5.4	6.4	8.0	8.5
Advancement	3.8	6.4	8.0	8.5
Role Clarity	6.3	7.0	8.0	8.5
Empowerment	6.4	7.0	8.0	8.5
Composite:	5.6	7.0	8.0	8.5

GOAL 1A2

Employee | 1A2 — • Improve Regional Employee Communications.

1A2 • Composite of employee satisfaction scores by 7.0 by year-end 1995, 8.0 by year-end 1996, and 8.5 by year-end 1997.

	94	95	96	97
Input	5.9	6.5	8.0	8.5
Clarity	6.3	7.0	8.0	8.5

(Continued)

Figure A2-3. Business Plan Alignment—Telecommunications.

205

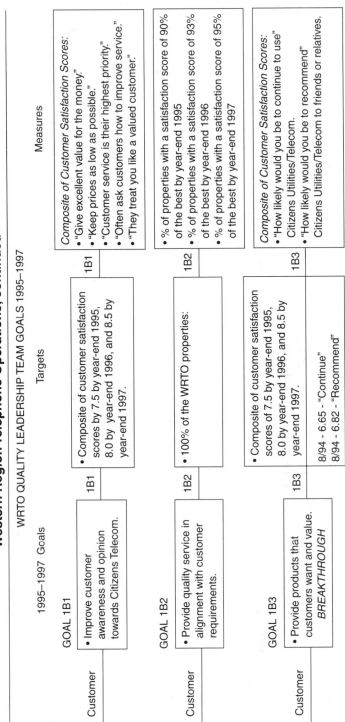

BUSINESS PLAN ALIGNMENT—TELECOMMUNICATIONS
Western Region Telephone Operations, continued

WRTO QUALITY LEADERSHIP TEAM GOALS 1995–1997

1995–1997 Goals	Targets	Measures
Customer — GOAL 1B1	1B1	1B1
• Improve customer awareness and opinion towards Citizens Telecom.	• Composite of customer satisfaction scores by 7.5 by year-end 1995, 8.0 by year-end 1996, and 8.5 by year-end 1997.	*Composite of Customer Satisfaction Scores:* • "Give excellent value for the money." • "Keep prices as low as possible." • "Customer service is their highest priority." • "Often ask customers how to improve service." • "They treat you like a valued customer."
Customer — GOAL 1B2	1B2	1B2
• Provide quality service in alignment with customer requirements.	• 100% of the WRTO properties:	• % of properties with a satisfaction score of 90% of the best by year-end 1995 • % of properties with a satisfaction score of 93% of the best by year-end 1996 • % of properties with a satisfaction score of 95% of the best by year-end 1997
Customer — GOAL 1B3	1B3	1B3
• Provide products that customers want and value. *BREAKTHROUGH*	• Composite of customer satisfaction scores of 7.5 by year-end 1995, 8.0 by year-end 1996, and 8.5 by year-end 1997. 8/94 - 6.65 - "Continue" 8/94 - 6.82 - "Recommend"	*Composite of Customer Satisfaction Scores:* • "How likely would you be to continue to use" Citizens Utilities/Telecom. • "How likely would you be to recommend" Citizens Utilities/Telecom to friends or relatives.

Figure A2-3. (*Continued*)

CORPORATE   SECTOR   DIVISION

GOAL 1

Goal 1 — Through Target Excellence, Citizens will be the employer and supplier of choice.

CUSTOMER

Goal 1a — The Energy Sector will be within 10% of the "Best" by year end 1996.
SPONSOR: Jim Avery

Goal 1a1 — KE's customer survey results will be within 14% of the "Best" by year-end 1995 and 10% of the "Best" by year-end 1996.
SPONSOR: Faye Akasaki

Goal 1b — The Electric Segment will improve outage hours to 2.9.
SPONSOR: Division

Goal 1b1 — KE will improve production outage hours to less than 60 for 12 months ended 12/31/95.
SPONSOR: Dan McCarthy

Goal 1b2 — KE will improve non-production outage hours to less than 2.3 for 12 months ended 12/31/95.
SPONSOR: Jack Leavitt

Goal 1c — Increase customer energy service value by $1.2 million through cost-effective DSM programs delivered to 5,000 customers within the Electric Segment.
SPONSOR: Sean Breen

Goal 1c1 — KE will implement 3 full-scale DSM programs by year-end 1995.
SPONSOR: Denny Polosky

Goal 1d — The Energy Sector will maintain O&M expenses less commodities per customer for 1995 at the 1994 level.
SPONSOR: Norman Bowley

Goal 1d1 — KE will maintain O&M less commodities per customer at less than $555 per customer.
SPONSORS: Kalindi Bhatt & Dept. Managers

EMPLOYEE

Goal 1e — The Energy Sector will close the gap between the current employee satisfaction index and 8.0 by 50 percent in 1995 and will achieve an employee satisfaction index of 8.0 by year-end 1996.
SPONSOR: Jim Avery

Goal 1e1 — KE will close the gap between the 1994 employee satisfaction index and 8.0 by 50% in 1995.
SPONSOR: Joan Zeglarski

Goal 1f — Develop and initiate an Energy Sector training plan which provides an average of 40 hours annually of training per employee by year-end 1995.

Goal 1f1 — This goal will be supported by the division but will not have a corresponding division goal.

Goal 1g — Develop and initiate an Energy Sector communication plan in 1995.
SPONSOR: Carolyn Colvard & Karen Bonnett

Goal 1g1 — This goal will be supported by the division but will not have a corresponding division goal.

Figure A2-4. 1995 Business Plan Energy Sector Goals—Kauai Electric.

207

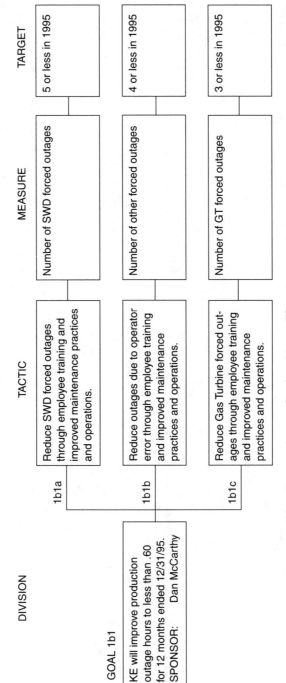

Figure A2-5. 1995 Business Plan Energy Sector Goals—Kauai Electric.

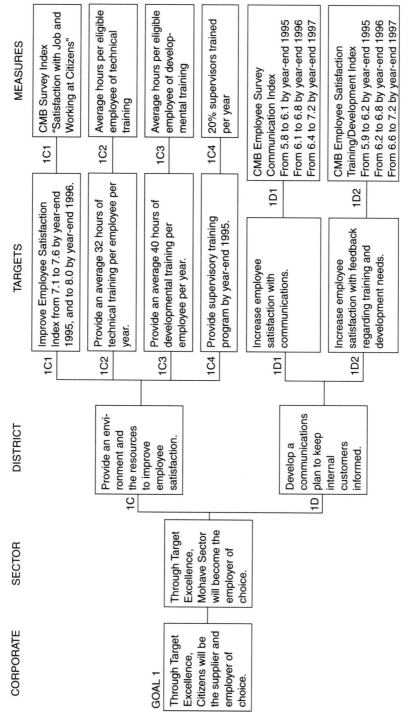

CORPORATE	SECTOR	DISTRICT	TARGETS		MEASURES

GOAL 1

Through Target Excellence, Citizens will be the supplier and employer of choice.

Through Target Excellence, Mohave Sector will become the employer of choice.

1C Provide an environment and the resources to improve employee satisfaction.

1C1 Improve Employee Satisfaction Index from 7.1 to 7.6 by year-end 1995, and to 8.0 by year-end 1996.

1C1 CMB Survey Index "Satisfaction with Job and Working at Citizens"

1C2 Provide an average 32 hours of technical training per employee per year.

1C2 Average hours per eligible employee of technical training

1C3 Provide an average 40 hours of developmental training per employee per year.

1C3 Average hours per eligible employee of developmental training

1C4 Provide supervisory training program by year-end 1995.

1C4 20% supervisors trained per year

1D Develop a communications plan to keep internal customers informed.

1D1 Increase employee satisfaction with communications.

1D1 CMB Employee Survey Communication Index
From 5.8 to 6.1 by year-end 1995
From 6.1 to 6.8 by year-end 1996
From 6.4 to 7.2 by year-end 1997

1D2 Increase employee satisfaction with feedback regarding training and development needs.

1D2 CMB Employee Satisfaction Training/Development Index
From 5.9 to 6.2 by year-end 1995
From 6.2 to 6.8 by year-end 1996
From 6.6 to 7.2 by year-end 1997

Figure A2-6. Citizens Utilities—Mohave Sector 1995 Business Plan.

3

Examples of Chairman's Review Questions

The review process is considered one of the key activities for aligning the organization from top to bottom. Moreover, when done well it can nurture and support a climate of learning and growing so vital in today's challenging business environment. Below are questions which the Chairman of Unum asks—and, by example, others ask throughout the company. We hope they will, with some slight modification, give you some ideas to incorporate in your reviews, wherever you work in your organization.

'98 GOALS CHAIRMAN'S REVIEW: EXAMPLES OF REVIEW TOPICS

Overall

- What is the overall level of understanding of the '98 Goals within the organization?
- What are the benchmarks for planned progress toward the '98 Goals?
- What are additional enterprise-wide support needs?
- What are the "best practices" which can be shared with other UNUM organizations?

People Goal

- What actions are being taken, and what are the results? What are the challenges to employee understanding?
- What are the measures used to assess the progress between corporate surveys ("real-time metrics")?
- What is the composition of agreement/disagreement statements, and how is this being addressed?

Customer Satisfaction

- What are the current dynamics of the marketplace? How is this changing UNUM's customer needs and satisfaction?

- How is the "voice of the customer" being heard? What are the measurements used to track customer satisfaction?
- What efforts are underway to better understand customer needs and provide "best value"?

Operating Effectiveness

- What steps are being taken to grow the top line?
- What are the key processes being worked on? Why were they selected? How do current efforts enhance value from the customer's perspective?
- What sharing/leveraging of strengths is taking place across the enterprise? What economies of scale are being realized?

Shareowner Value

- Discuss ROE target, trends if appropriate.

4

Customer-Focus Audit

The following questionnaire (Table A4-1) gives you an opportunity to assess the degree to which your organization is focused on your customers. Analysis of your answers will help you better align your strategy, processes, and people with customer needs.

INSTRUCTIONS

For each question, rate your organization on the extent to which you think it is customer focused. Use the 0-to-10-point scale, with 0 indicating no customer focus and 10 indicating total customer focus. Circle

Table A4-1. Your Customer-Focus Audit.

Total Customer Focus		
To what extent . . .	**Not at all**	**Totally**
1. Does your organization encourage continuous communication with customers?	0 1 2 3 4 5 6 7 8 9 10	
2. Is customer data gathered by everyone in your organization?	0 1 2 3 4 5 6 7 8 9 10	
3. Does responsibility for customer satisfaction belong to everyone in your organization?	0 1 2 3 4 5 6 7 8 9 10	
4. Do employees have the authority to solve customer problems?	0 1 2 3 4 5 6 7 8 9 10	
5. Are customer needs used to drive the things your organization does?	0 1 2 3 4 5 6 7 8 9 10	
6. Is customer information communicated throughout your organization?	0 1 2 3 4 5 6 7 8 9 10	
7. Is customer satisfaction based on actual customer data?	0 1 2 3 4 5 6 7 8 9 10	
8. Are measurements of effectiveness focused on satisfying unstated customer needs?	0 1 2 3 4 5 6 7 8 9 10	

the number that corresponds to your response. The higher your scores, the more likely you have a customer-driven organization.

5

Traditional versus Total Customer Focus

The chart below contrasts the way organizations used to focus on their customers with the way world-class organizations organize around their customers. On the following pages are examples of how organizations align their key processes and systems to provide outstanding service and products.

Table A5-1. Traditional versus Total Customer Focus.

The graphic below compares traditional customer focus with total customer focus.

	Traditional Customer Focus	Total Customer Focus
Communication with customers is	Complaint or problem based	Continuous, multidimensional, solicited, and encouraged
Customer data is gathered by	Strategists or specialists	Everyone in the organization, with a lead role assigned to employees with direct customer contact
Responsibility for customer satisfaction belongs to	Customer service departments	Everyone in the organization, starting with senior management and cascading down
Customer problems are solved by	Strict, preset policies and procedures	Employees who are given the authority to act on behalf of the customer within defined boundaries
Customer needs are interpreted by	Strategists, specialists, or top levels of management	People throughout the organization, with the voice of the customer driving everything they do
Feedback mechanisms are	Preset, static, supplier focused	Continuous, dynamic, and driven by customer data
Customer satisfaction is defined by	Complaints or problems	Continuous improvement based on actual customer data
Measurements of effectiveness are	Internally focused	Focused on satisfying the unstated needs of the customer

Table A5-2. Examples from Total Customer Focus Organizations.

	Total Customer Focus
Communication with customers is continuous, multidimensional, solicited, and encouraged.	**A financial research service uses every opportunity to gather, interpret, and build on customer information.** This research service is in constant contact with outside organizations. In addition to collecting the data required for current services, it also gathers information on where and how it can enhance its range of services and thus its competitive advantage.
Customer data is gathered by everyone in the organization, with a lead role assigned to employees with direct customer contact.	**A national brokerage firm continuously gathers information on customer preferences from client calls.** In addition to taking orders, service representatives and brokers seek data on customer perceptions, reactions, and desires.
Responsibility for customer satisfaction belongs to everyone in the organization, starting with senior management and cascading down.	**In one national hotel chain, the CEO receives customer comment cards regularly and relays his reactions and suggestions to individual hotels.** He also visits the hotels and formally communicates the results of his visits to the entire organization.
Customer problems are solved by employees who are given the authority to act on behalf of the customer within defined boundaries.	**A national restaurant chain has given its service staff the authority to replace any disputed order.** Rather than needing approval from a manager or supervisor, the staff has clear standards for returning a meal, no questions asked, and bringing the customer the correct order. The standards establish that in many cases the customer will get his or her meal on the house.
Customer needs are interpreted by people throughout the organization, with the voice of the customer driving everything they do.	**A major printer of bank checks has led the industry in innovations, such as scenic checks, for years.** The salespeople have kept closely attuned to customer needs. And the company has developed a system for conveying the salesperson's input directly into the company's business strategy.

(Continued)

Table A5-2. Examples from Total Customer Focus Organizations (*Continued*)

	Total Customer Focus
Feedback mechanisms are continuous, dynamic, and driven by customer data.	**An international travel-services organization constantly checks and responds to data about customer requests for information.** When customers regularly call for a certain type of information or service, the company quickly establishes a formal system that supplies what is requested. This reduces rework and increases customer satisfaction.
Customer satisfaction is defined by continuous improvement based on actual customer data.	**A large, urban children's hospital provides low-cost housing for patients' families.** Interviews and surveys revealed that many patients were bothered by the lack of convenient accommodations for their families. By acquiring nearby real estate and converting it to low-cost, short-term housing, the hospital has reduced patient anxiety, thereby increasing satisfaction.
Measurements of effectiveness are focused on satisfying the unstated needs of the customer.	**Some automobile dealerships have established a policy of providing "personal" mechanics to strengthen customer relationships.** Research showed that dealership repair shops frequently lost customers to smaller, more personal maintenance and repair shops. So these dealerships have changed the way they schedule and assign work. As part of the new policy, mechanics are rewarded and recognized primarily based on feedback solicited directly from their personal customers.

6

UNUM's Critical
Success Factors
and Goals

In Figure 6-1, for simplicity of discussion, we provided an abbreviated, edited version of UNUM's four critical success factors. In the following pages we present the actual documents that are communicated throughout the organization as a means of ensuring vertical alignment.

UNUM PEOPLE

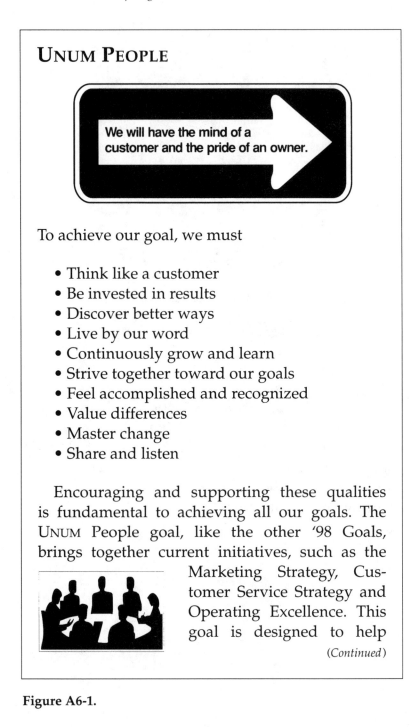

We will have the mind of a customer and the pride of an owner.

To achieve our goal, we must

- Think like a customer
- Be invested in results
- Discover better ways
- Live by our word
- Continuously grow and learn
- Strive together toward our goals
- Feel accomplished and recognized
- Value differences
- Master change
- Share and listen

Encouraging and supporting these qualities is fundamental to achieving all our goals. The UNUM People goal, like the other '98 Goals, brings together current initiatives, such as the Marketing Strategy, Customer Service Strategy and Operating Excellence. This goal is designed to help

(Continued)

Figure A6-1.

each of us close the distance between the company we are and the company we want to be.

To become that company, we must *think like a customer* and *feel the pride of an owner* in

- Our company
- Our Vision and Values
- What we do
- How we do it

Measurement

 A benchmark survey will integrate the elements of the Operating Excellence and Speak Up! surveys into a tool for gauging our progress.

Metric

 Our goal is to improve annually on the score established by the benchmark survey. In addition, we will monitor our progress toward this goal on an ongoing basis through formal and informal gathering of employee opinions.

Figure A6-1. (*Continued*)

OPERATING EFFECTIVENESS

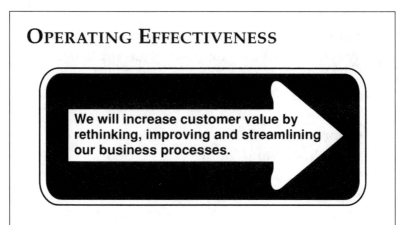

We will increase customer value by rethinking, improving and streamlining our business processes.

This goal will improve overall effectiveness, not just reduce expenses, both of which are crucial to generating sustained superior performance.

The focus on improvement is driven by the Speak Up! Survey results, other employee feedback and increasing competitive pressures.

Bending Over Backwards!

This is how we achieved the 6-15-92 goal one year ahead of schedule! And, it's precisely the way we will meet our Operating Effectiveness goal and each of our '98 Goals. We will succeed only with the commitment of every member of the UNUM team. And, we will look to each other—every UNUM employee—for leadership and creativity in improving our operating processes.

Figure A6-1. (*Continued*)

The way to improved operating effectiveness is reducing our ratio of expenses to premiums or revenue. This calls for, among other things, constantly seeking creative solutions for improving our processes. The result is a more efficient, more effective organization that consistently does the "right things right."

Reducing our expense ratio will improve our competitiveness and increase earnings.

Measurement

Operating costs will grow at no more than one-half the rate of premium or revenue growth.

Metric

By 1998, our total operating costs ratio will be reduced by approximately one-third.

Figure A6-1. (*Continued*)

CUSTOMER SATISFACTION

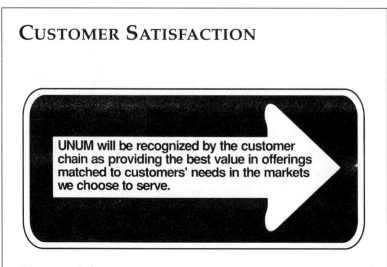

UNUM will be recognized by the customer chain as providing the best value in offerings matched to customers' needs in the markets we choose to serve.

This goal focuses on our customers' perception of overall value. Establishing a goal based on achieving what the customer views as superior value will allow us to achieve maximum customer satisfaction.

Value is the key determinant in influencing purchasing decisions. Value must be created, delivered and perceived along the entire customer chain. Improving customers' perceived value of UNUM's offerings will result in increased market share through new sales, improved persistency and greater customer-generated recommendations. This outcome is critical to achieving sustained superior performance and worldwide leadership.

Figure A6-1. (*Continued*)

Customer Satisfaction is:

- Putting our customers first in all that we do
- Listening carefully to find out what they really want
- Anticipating what they need
- Meeting, even exceeding their needs and expectations in all of our contacts and with all of our products and services

Measurement

Each UNUM area with an external customer chain will develop a customer value measurement tool. It will be aimed at determining our customers' assessment of the overall value of our products and services.

Metric

We will continuously improve our customers' perception of the value of UNUM's offerings so that the number of customers who *do not* rate UNUM "very good" or "excellent" will have improved (declined) by 40 percent when we compile our final measurements in 1998.

Figure A6-1. (*Continued*)

SHAREHOLDER VALUE

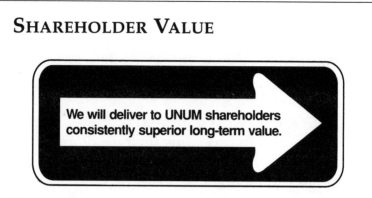

We will deliver to UNUM shareholders consistently superior long-term value.

This goal focuses on shareholders: the investors who purchase UNUM stock and thereby provide much of the capital for company operations and business expansion.

Shareholder value embodies what investors are seeking: a superior return on the money they invest in UNUM.

By making Shareholder Value a goal, we have given investors, stockbrokers and financial analysts a "yardstick" by which UNUM's progress toward its other stated goals can be measured. Companies that meet their goals win favor with investors and thereby enjoy a more favorable capital position.

What Are Investors Looking For?

They are looking for a superior return on their investment.

The key components of superior investment performance (total return) are dividends and

Figure A6-1. (*Continued*)

the appreciation of UNUM's stock price. Dividends are per-share payments made by the company to its shareholders.

Measurement

 The measurement for this goal is total return (dividends plus share price appreciation).

Metric

 We will achieve a total return to shareholders that consistently places UNUM among the top 125 companies listed on the Standard & Poor's 500.

To get there, UNUM is aiming for an ROE of 18 percent by 1998, assuming stability in capital markets and our financial requirements. ROE (return on equity) is the rate a business earns on its net worth.

Figure A6-1. (*Continued*)

7

The Dynamics of the Self-Aligning Organization

Figure A7-1 shows the key elements in the alignment model that interact in an ongoing way with each other. Next to each element are the actions that are required to ensure that each part is performing its critical function while linking to the other parts of the system. For example, "Strategy" requires that a strategic vision is created that is shared by people at every level and function within the organization (see Chapter 4). The sharing comes about through a process that gets people from different parts of the organization literally into a room to analyze data and draw conclusions. As this strategic vision is deployed down into the organization, key strategic work processes are identified and aligned with the vision. A key element in ensuring that the organization stays

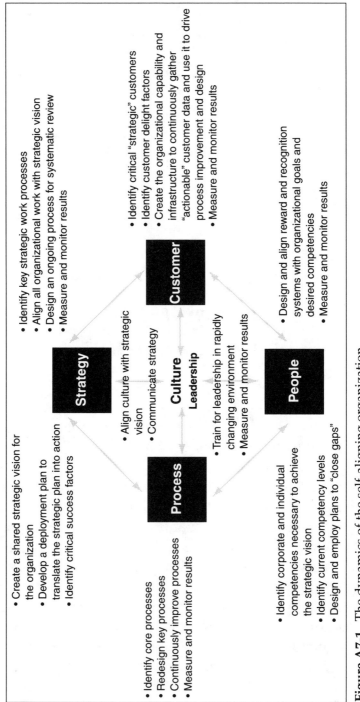

- Create a shared strategic vision for the organization
- Develop a deployment plan to translate the strategic plan into action
- Identify critical success factors

- Identify key strategic work processes
- Align all organizational work with strategic vision
- Design an ongoing process for systematic review
- Measure and monitor results

Strategy

- Identify critical "strategic" customers
- Identify customer delight factors
- Create the organizational capability and infrastructure to continuously gather "actionable" customer data and use it to drive process improvement and design
- Measure and monitor results

Customer

- Align culture with strategic vision
- Communicate strategy

Culture

Leadership

- Train for leadership in rapidly changing environment
- Measure and monitor results

Process

People

- Identify core processes
- Redesign key processes
- Continuously improve processes
- Measure and monitor results

- Identify corporate and individual competencies necessary to achieve the strategic vision
- Identify current competency levels
- Design and employ plans to "close gaps"

- Design and align reward and recognition systems with organizational goals and desired competencies
- Measure and monitor results

Figure A7-1. The dynamics of the self-aligning organization.

aligned is the development and use of a systematic re-view process that measures and monitors results (see Chapter 6).

The "Customer" element requires that strategic cus-tomers are identified before any work can be done on improving customer satisfaction (see Chapter 5). If you are striving to build market share, for example, then you will want to ensure that everyone in the orga-nization is clear as to the purpose of the strategy, and how the satisfaction of a particular customer group is crucial to the strategy. Then you create the organiza-tional capability to drive improvements in the key areas that customers care most about. And to stay aligned, you must constantly measure and monitor results.

The "Process" element requires the identification of the core processes that support the strategy; the con-tinual improvement—and if necessary redesign—of these processes as defined by the strategy and cus-tomers (see Chapter 5); and the measuring and moni-toring of results against the customer requirements and the strategy.

The "People" element has several components that together enable the self-aligning organization to un-leash the enormous potential that resides in its people. First you need to identify corporate and individual competencies necessary to achieve the strategic vision. Competency levels need to be set, along with activities for providing required training and support systems. Finally, reward and recognition systems need to be aligned with organizational goals and desired compe-tencies (see Chapter 6). These activities need be mea-sured continually to ensure people will have the re-quired skills to implement and sustain changes in strategy and/or processes.

"Culture" becomes the playing field that enables or inhibits rapid realignment to occur in response to changes in the business environment. To ensure that the culture supports flexibility and resiliency, people all over the organization need training in a competency that is becoming more and more critical—the competency in leading people so that they can work productively in a fast-changing, complex world (see Chapter 7). This requires aligning the culture of the organization as well as the subcultures within departments and even workgroups with strategic goals. And, of course, communication becomes a never-ending activity to enable the organization to respond to new information.

Notes

Chapter 1

[1] Michael Hammer and James Champy, *Reengineering the Corporation* (New York: HarperCollins, 1993), 5.

[2] Michael Hammer, *The Wall Street Journal*, 26 November 1996.

[3] "Restructuring Out and Growth In," *The Wall Street Journal*, 9 December 1996.

Chapter 2

[1] "Cracks in Quality," *The Economist*, 18 April 1992, p. 67.

[2] We use the term "process" liberally in this book. If you are unfamiliar with the term, we offer Hammer and Champy's definition, which is as good as any: "We define a business process as a collection of activities that takes one or more kinds of input and creates an output that is of value to the customer." Michael Ham-

mer and James Champy, *Reenginnering the Corporation* (New York: HarperBusiness, 1993), 35.

[3] Paul Lawrence and Jay Lorsch, *Organization and Environment* (Homewood, Ill.: Richard D. Irwin, 1969), 11.

[4] Michael A. Verespej, "Flying His Own Course," *Industry Week*, 20 November 1995, 23.

[5] *Far Eastern Economic Review* 160, no. 1 (26 December 1996).

Chapter 3

[1] Gregory H. Watson, *Strategic Benchmarking* (New York: John Wiley & Sons, 1993), 131–132.

[2] James M. Utterback, *Mastering the Dynamics of Innovation* (Boston, Mass.: Harvard Business School Press, 1994).

Chapter 4

[1] Vincent P. Barabba, *Meeting of the Minds* (Boston, Mass.: Harvard Business School Press, 1995), 197. The dialogue decision process described in Barabba is explained further in James Matheson and David Matheson, *The Smart Organization* (Boston, Mass.: Harvard Business School Press, 1997).

Chapter 5

[1] Dava Sobel, *Longitude* (New York: Walker, 1995), 4.

[2] Robert J. Keith, "The Marketing Revolution," *Journal of Marketing* 24, no 1 (January 1960): 38. For a full discussion of the rise of the "market concept," see also Vincent P. Barabba, *Meeting of the Minds* (Boston, Mass.: Harvard Business School Press, 1995), 43–69, and Frederick E. Webster, Jr., *Market-Driven Management* (New York: John Wiley & Sons, 1994).

[3] G. Stalk, Jr. and A.M. Webber, "Japan's Dark Side of Time," *Harvard Business Review*, July 1993.

[4] George Labovitz, "Keeping Your Internal Customers Satisfied," *The Wall Street Journal*, 6 July 1987.

[5] See George Labovitz, Charlie Chang, and Victor Rosansky, *Making Quality Work* (New York: Harvard Business School Press, 1993), 81–83.

Chapter 6

[1] Robert S. Kaplan and David P. Norton, "The Balanced Scorecard: Measures That Drive Performance," *Harvard Business Review,* January-February 1992, 71–79. See also "Using the Balanced Scorecard as a Strategic Management System," *Harvard Business Review,* January-February 1996, 75–85, and *The Balanced Scorecard* (Boston, Mass.: Harvard Business School Press, 1996), by the same authors.
[2] "A Third Generation Galvin Moves Up," *Forbes,* 30 April 1990, 57.

Chapter 7

[1] James Belasco and Ralph Stayer, *Flight of the Buffalo* (New York: Warner Books, 1993), 18.
[2] Gordon R. Sullivan and Michael V. Harper, *Hope Is Not a Method* (New York: Times Business, 1996), 213.
[3] Dwight Gertz and Joao Baptista, *Grow to Be Great* (New York: Free Press, 1995), 102.
[4] Michael A. Verespej, "Flying His Own Course," *Industry Week,* 20 November 1995, 22–23.
[5] Gertz and Baptista, *Grow to Be Great,* 154–155.
[6] Verespej, "Flying His Own Course," 22–23.
[7] John Kotter, *The General Managers* (New York: Free Press, 1982).

Index